Bread and Roses

10 0384768 5

Bread and Roses

Written by Paul Laverty

Directed by Ken Loach

First published in 2001
by ScreenPress Books
28 Castle Street Eye Suffolk IP23 7AW

Photoset by Parker Typesetting Service, Leicester
Printed by Clays Ltd, St Ives plc

A CIP record for this book
is available from the British Library

ISBN 1 901680 49 5

For more information on forthcoming ScreenPress Books
contact the publishers at:

ScreenPress Books
28 Castle Street
Eye Suffolk
IP23 7AW
or fax: 01379 870 261
www.screenpress.co.uk
mail@screenpress.co.uk

2 4 6 8 19 9 7 5 3 1

Contents

Foreword

Bread and Roses is that rare film in which the struggles of ordinary people come to life with explosive power and passion. At a time when there is fulsome self-congratulation in the United States about the wonders of the economy, here we have the reality of 'the other America'. It is the America of working people, many of them immigrants, most of them women, who clean the offices of the rich in silence and apparent acceptance – until one day they rebel. The acting in this film is extraordinary, the dialogue as real and earthy as life itself, the direction superb. I hope it will be widely seen, because it can shock viewers into an awareness of a world that is invisible to most.

Howard Zinn, August 2000

Introduction

This story started in the autumn of 1994 when I lived in a funny green house just off MacArthur Park in downtown Los Angeles. From outside it looked like something from a Grimm's fairytale. From inside it felt a bit like *Alice in Wonderland*. In its youth it must have been an elegant merchant house with rich owners. Now, in decaying splendour, each of its rooms was rented out to mostly single men.

Downtown LA is like Central America in the middle of Los Angeles. Most of the white men in the green house didn't want to be there and often displayed barely disguised contempt for those with whom they shared their lives.

One spent all day photocopying, all night in front of a TV, with a trip to Disneyland on his birthday to break the routine. Another lived out in the back garden and had converted the garage into living quarters. He occasionally gave drum lessons to Asian students, which had grown in his own mind to a jazz school. The guy below me played the same Country and Western record each evening, which he accompanied on his electric guitar, and talked about his forthcoming record deal. To prove the point he displayed soft-focus self-portraits in a wheat field dressed as a cowboy. Another man along the corridor yodelled upside down between two chairs as he played the violin and hoped to be spotted as he entertained on Santa Monica boardwalk. The tale of the muscular transvestite and the Brazilian whose father was once an assassin for his country's security forces will take too long to tell, so when they found out I was there to write a screenplay about Latino janitors nobody batted an eyelid.

The rest of the house was filled with recently arrived Mexicans or other Latin Americans who had crossed the border in all manner of strange and wonderful adventures.

At night-time in the green house returning workers would bring in their car batteries in the same way executives might bring in their laptops and line them up in the hallway on top of old newspaper. The grease and oil still filtered through and stained the once beautiful dark wooden floors.

Night-time had its own noises. It is an LA cliché to talk of popping guns and all the madness within earshot but beyond the imagination. There was an El Salvadorean gang around the corner selling drugs which appeared like a parody of gangs in a hundred films. It wasn't so much the pencil moustaches, the tattoos, the white vests to emphasize muscle and torso, that somehow struck me as strangely comic, but the three-quarter-length pants that inevitably hung at half-mast. But it wasn't funny. One evening I passed them on vigil. There was a flickering candle on the pavement beside and open bottle of Corona beer, a portrait of the Virgin of Guadaloup and a black and white photograph of one of their own who had been shot dead in a drive-by.

There were other noises around the green house. Cruising clients would drive down our street to eye up ageing prostitutes. (One, six months pregnant, was a regular sitting on our front step. Dressed in a pink floral dress and obviously suffering from AIDS, she asked me if I wanted a good time.) Vibrations from their vehicles coming too close would set off car alarms on parked cars which still had their batteries and the endless cycle of noise would continue.

There was also a strange metallic crunching sound that became so familiar. From the porch, at first sight, it looked surreal. Shopping trolleys hovered towards us, filled with discarded drinks cans, glistening under the neon lights as if powered by themselves. Only as they rattled closer could I identify ghostly dark figures of the homeless pushing along the fruits of their search which would earn them a few dollars from recycling centres.

Not as frequent but more disturbing was the sound of mad people who wandered the streets.

To these familiar decibels of exploitation and self-destruction, typical of many inner cities around the world, were added the tambourines of an Evangelical church which proclaimed a better tomorrow as they praised the Lord. 'O Sweet Jesus . . .'

In the midst of all this, as usual, were families getting on with their lives in a daily routine as best they could. Poverty isn't neutral. It is corrosive and vicious. One of the women who lived with us would take a knife from her bag and keep it in her hand on the short walk from the bus stop to her home. Most of the occupants in the green house had their own mugging horror story to tell and my cowboy friend was nearly murdered during my stay. Lack of sleep, badly paid temporary work, fear outside the front door and tension within, all worked together to form a powerful cocktail which wore people down.

But not everybody took to drugs and tambourines. Some got angry. It was the sheer energy and imagination of another response, in this same community, which drew me to the janitors of Los Angeles.

The history of the Justice for Janitors Campaign is explained elsewhere. But from the very beginning several things struck me about the janitors themselves, the union organizers who worked with them and their string of community volunteers.

Despite what seemed like impossible odds, these people exhibited remarkable confidence. Nobody here was playing some sentimental notion of downtrodden victim. Nobody believed anything was going to change unless they did it for and by themselves; there was a roll up your sleeves, get the work done now and stop moaning atmosphere.

There was a clarity about how corporations functioned and how they could be confronted. This required detailed research of company ownership; perhaps a pension fund, sometimes a union pension fund, was involved, with a forthcoming AGM organised, where company abuses could be highlighted to everyone's embarassment; or zoning laws might provide a weak spot if the target companies were planning new buildings in other parts of the city, or perhaps tax breaks were open to challenge. There were endless possibilities, so they had to make strategic use of their limited resources. At another level blocking off just one exit from a freeway could cause chaos in the banks and offices downtown.

Confidence, like optimism, is highly contagious when mixed with hard work. So it spread.

xi

Oscars ceremonies, Thanksgiving, leading Hollywood talent agencies based in the same building as a new non-union contract, or whatever was in the air, gave them lots of ammunition to mount powerful counter-images to 'the American dream' which masked obscene polarization of wealth and influence. I remember one march along Rodeo Drive, the shopping centre in the heart of Beverly Hills. Despite all the noise, banners (Luxury by Day, Sweat Shop by Night), drums, police and media, the most unforgettable image was the simple contrast in size. Short brown cleaners. Tall white shoppers.

Getting to know how the campaign worked was one thing, but getting to know the cleaners and their families was another. One face sticks in my mind. She was a mother from Guatemala. With her entire savings from two and a half years' baby-sitting, she paid Coyotes to bring up her two children from Guatemala. They made it across the border into Mexico. (Sebastiao Salgado's wonderful book of photographs, *Exodus*, opens with a stunning vista of the border crossing over the River Suchiate.) They took two weeks to pass through Mexico but got caught at the border on the US side. Her children, whom she hadn't seen since they were infants, were repatriated. Their mother started again. Two and half years' more baby-sitting of other people's children. Two and half years' saving, but the next time she got them through.

These and other stories were told with a simple matter-of-factness. (People were amazed to hear I had filled out my visa waiver for free on a flight to LA which cost only a few hundred pounds.) Little surprise therefore that threats of deportation for union organizing were so frightening to many cleaners who didn't have their papers. Many were repaying family members who had got them across in the first place, as well as sending money home to Central America.

I met cleaners and supporters who had the most extraordinary lives. Some were ex-students from El Salvador who fought in the civil war, others had experience in Nicaragua during the 1980s, others came from the Guatemalan countryside or Mexican shanty towns. The diversity of human experience was endless. The irony was that once they put on a cleaner's uniform they were all treated exactly the same; as one of them told me, 'You become invisible.' It does take a monstrous arrogance and breathtaking ignorance to assume that these lives are somehow less interesting than those of the lawyers and agents who work in the very same offices during day-light hours.

One thing that struck home was that many of the cleaners had two jobs, and for those who worked weekends, sometimes three. They would do their cleaning work from 6 p.m. until 2 a.m. and then have a day job too, which put incredible stress on those caring for children. Many were scared that their kids, if left unsupervised, would join the street gangs, but it was impossible to bring up a family with just the income from a cleaning job.

During this time I was lucky enough to come across *A People's History of the United States* written by Howard Zinn; an antidote to the sentimentality of one president after another citing God and 'the American people'. It never romanticizes immigrants, slaves, Indians, women or workers, but opens up a continuous history of resistance in the face of hideous violence.

I read of mill workers in 1835 going on strike to reduce their working day from thirteen and half a hours to eleven hours. I learned about the 100,000 workers in New York who after a three months' strike won the right to an eight-hour day in 1872. And here we were in tinsel town, home to the stars, fast approaching the year 2000, with many workers back to combined shifts in excess of fourteen hours again.

Little wonder there was trouble.

Los Angeles, Century City, Avenue of the Stars, 16 June 1990. To cut a long story short, Los Angeles Police Department decided to teach these upstart janitors a lesson. Century City houses some of the most prestigious office blocks in Los Angeles. It is full of media companies, Hollywood agents and other high-flyers. It was also the battleground between union organizers and a multinational cleaning company hiring non union-workers on short-term contracts, with the critical consequence that non-union workers were not entitled to health coverage for themselves or their families, to say nothing of rates of pay and other rights like holidays.

The marchers and the police met on Avenue of the Stars. Fortunately someone had a video, and we have used some real footage in the film. Many were beaten up, several suffered serious injuries and one woman had a miscarriage. There was such an outcry that it led to the union's biggest breakthrough and the cleaning companies backed down.

Since then the janitors have continued to organize and following city-wide protests with huge public sympathy they signed a master contract in April 2000 which has had a knock-on effect on other low-paid workers in the whole of LA county. Tens of thousands of workers and their families now have health care. It doesn't change the world, but it transforms their lives.

We got the film shot at the end of '99 in just thirty days, which was an incredible feat by the team. It was cut in the first months of 2000. It was invited to the Cannes film festival in May, where it got a very generous response from the audience dressed in obligatory fine gowns and evening suits. I kept thinking what the cleaners might make of all this in their uniforms.

Los Angeles, Century City, Avenue of the Stars, 16 June, 2000. Ten years to the day from when the cleaners were beaten up, in the middle of the afternoon, timed to finish so janitors could start their shifts, the union and Lions Gate distribution company organized the US premiere of *Bread and Roses* in a cinema on Avenue of the Stars. Many of those who had lived through these events now watched themselves on screen. It was a premiere with a running commentary: jokes, laughter and applause for friends they recognized.

In trying to tell this story I found myself identifying with Zinn's approach to history: 'I don't want to invent victories for people's movements. But to think that history-writing must aim simply to recapitulate the failures that dominate the past is to make historians collaborators in an endless cycle of defeat. If history is to be creative, to anticipate a possible future without denying the past, it should, I believe, emphasize new possibilities by disclosing those hidden episodes of the past when, even if in brief flashes, people showed their ability to resist, to join together, occasionally to win. I am supposing, or perhaps only hoping, that our future may be found in the past's fugitive moments of compassion rather in its solid centuries of warfare.'

I went back to the green house. Many people had moved on but I met my cowboy friend, who still rented the same room. You won't believe it, he said, I had a little romance with one of the Kennedys. You won't believe it, I said, but we made our film.

Paul Laverty, December 2000

Bread and Roses

VAN. FREEWAY. DAY

Stoic Latino faces in the back of a van. Three adults and two youngsters (a boy and girl aged twelve and ten). Mariachi music booms from cheap speakers.

Maya (mid-twenties) wipes the sweat and dust from her face as she stares out at the passing countryside and a sign for Los Angeles.

Up front, two Coyotes (men who earn their living by illegally transporting people across the border). The driver (Coyote 1) is thick-set and powerful, while the other (Coyote 2), in the passenger seat, is immaculately dressed.

Maya leans her head on the window.

    TITLES.

FACES IN VAN MIXED WITH STACCATO FLASHBACKS OF
SCRUB-LAND. DAWN

Tiny dots in the distance scurry between two hills.

Same faces. Exertion and fear. They struggle to keep up with athletic young Coyote 1, who forces them on through the bush.

COYOTE 1
(all in Spanish)

Move your fucking ass and keep your heads down!

Scrambling feet on shale. Steep slope.

The young girl trips and falls heavily. Her older brother pulls her up. Shock on the girl's face from fall and Coyote's aggression.

Move it or I'll leave you here to rot!

3

Maya helps the girl and wipes dust and dirt from her clothes, while exchanging a filthy look with Coyote.

> MAYA
> *(to girl)*
> Don't you worry. OK.

She takes the girl's hand and moves on.

> COYOTE I
> *(to Maya as she passes)*
> Think this is a picnic, sweetheart?

> MAYA
> No ... but I think you're a dick.

They rush on.

They approach a dirt track and crouch down among the bushes. A border patrol Jeep throws up a trail of dust as it speeds by. They run across.

Splashing over a rocky stream.

They struggle to the brow of a hill. Heaving chests. Frightened faces streaked in sweat. They look down on to a built-up area.

INSIDE THE VAN

Still the mariachi music as they now trundle along the slow lane on the 110 Freeway towards downtown LA. Thousands of vehicles snake their way north and south.

Maya exchanges glances with the brother of the girl. She is now fast asleep, head leaning on his lap.

Maya and young boy stare out in wonder. Enormous office blocks, like some fairyland, shimmer in the distance, silhouetted against the San Gabriel Mountains. Bigger, taller, brighter and ever closer.

Maya unfolds a scrap of paper and stares down at an address. She rolls it up and hides it away again. She fidgets with a small statue of the Virgin of Guadalupe.

4

*Coyote 1 swings into a packed lane and heads for an exit. Horn!
Then the sudden acceleration of an expensive car that swishes past.
An angry face mouths expletives and gives the finger. The Coyotes
don't bat an eyelid.*

*Ever closer to these enormous monuments of corporate power
blazing their identity: First Interstate Bank, Union Bank, Citycorp,
Sanawa Bank, Arco Oil Company, Imperial Bank.*

INTO DOWNTOWN

*Sheer scale and spectacle of black shiny glass and chrome draw the
eye. Ghostly black figures rattle by, pushing recycled cans, glass or
bundles of old clothes in bright steel shopping trolleys, occasionally
silhouetted before plate glass, plush receptions, manicured plants
and stylized lighting behind waterfalls.*

*The cassette completes the cycle and starts up again from the
beginning with same identifiable pumping trumpets of the
mariachi.*

MAYA
(*all Spanish*)
Mother of God! How many fucking times you going to play
that!

COYOTE 1

Shut it!

*Coyote 2 turns rounds to look at her, intrigued. He has a big smile.
He turns down the music, much to the driver's annoyance.*

Fucking bitch.

MAYA

Fucking donkey.

Coyote 2 bursts out laughing, which annoys Coyote 1 even more.

*Off round another corner. More monuments to man's architectural
brilliance.*

Smell of poverty. Lots of people, but only black and brown faces. More homeless with trolleys. Down towards MacArthur Park. Central America in the middle of Los Angeles.

The van pulls into a private spot beside an excited huddle. Passengers, especially the children, stare out in wonder at their families. Nervous delight and shouts of recognition.

Coyote 2 opens the door, but blocks the exit. Rolled-up dollars are grabbed from the relatives and snapped into order and counted in a flash. On each transaction a body tumbles from the van and joins excited relatives.

The children jump from the van and are enthusiastically embraced.

Suddenly Maya's worried face catches sight of Rosa (mid-thirties though she looks older, tough but attractive) rushing towards them.

MAYA
(all Spanish)

Rosa! Rosa! I thought you weren't coming . . .

ROSA

Maya . . . are you OK?

They kiss through the window. Maya tries to push her way past the Coyote, but he blocks her path.

COYOTE 2

Money!

Maya recognizes the panic on Rosa's face as she hands over some cash. The Coyote counts it quickly.

Some kind of fucking joke . . . Where's the rest?

ROSA

I got robbed . . . Take my watch . . .

(*handing it over*)
I promise I'll pay the rest ... Give me a week ... Here's my
address! Please! You can trust me ... On my mother's life ...
You can trust me!

COYOTE 2

Fuck off!

MAYA
(*struggling*)
Rosa! Rosa! Get your hands off!

Coyote 1 roughly grabs Maya and throws her back into the van.

COYOTE 1
Fucking bitch! Get in there and shut it!

Rosa now pushes forward.

ROSA
Please ... let her go ...
(*pulling a ring off her finger*)
Take my ring ... my wedding ring! ... It's gold ...

Coyote 2 grabs it.

Please ... I beg you ...

*Maya comes out fighting harder. Coyote 1 grabs her again. Maya
knees him in the balls and he doubles up, swearing like hell, but
he's still hanging on to her. Coyote 2 throws her violently into the
van once more. He pulls out a knife.*

COYOTE 2
I'll cut your fucking throat.

ROSA
Don't touch her! Please ... I'll do anything ... anything!

The commotion has drawn the attention of passers-by.

COYOTE 1
(*still suffering*)
Let's get the hell out of here.

ROSA
Take me instead ...

COYOTE 1
Fucking crazy bitches!

Coyote 2 slams the door shut. Maya and Rosa are face to face through the glass. Coyote 1 starts up the engine.

Rosa runs alongside the van.

ROSA
Maya! Maya!

Van accelerates off. Rosa is overcome.

Coyote 2 examines Maya and then smiles at the driver, who is groaning slightly and rubbing his crotch.

COYOTE 2
How are your balls, Tarzan?

COYOTE 1
Feel like fucking coconuts ...
(*catching sight of her in the mirror*)
Mad cow!

Coyote 2 turns in his seat and lingers over Maya.

COYOTE 2
Lively little pussycat ... Right ... Back to Tijuana ... Or do I get a little company for a few days?

ROOM. PRINCE EDWARD. DOWNTOWN

Maya and Coyote 2 walk along the corridor in a dingy hotel. He takes her arm. She pulls away.

COYOTE 2

(*all Spanish*)

Relax ... I'm not like the other dick ... I got charm ... I want you to have a good time too.

They enter the room. He pulls her to him. Maya stands stiffly as she stares out over his shoulder. After a moment, she puts her hands round him too.

That's better ... Easy!

MAYA

You ain't as ugly as I thought ... but you smell bad.

COYOTE 2

Come on ... honest sweat.

MAYA

Get a wash ... and if you shave ... you might get lucky ... Move it!

She shoves him back on the bed and helps him pull off his spectacular cowboy boots.

COYOTE 2

Best boots in Mexico ... Cost me $300!

He undoes his shirt. He looks at her slyly, then locks the door and slips the key in his trouser pocket. He moves into the bathroom and turns on the shower as he hangs his trousers up on a hook.

Maya checks the window, but they are too high up. The adjoining balcony is too distant. Her eyes dart round the room.

MAYA

Can you sing?

COYOTE 2

Sure I can sing ... What would you like?

She walks back to the bathroom and swishes a dirty curtain a few

9

inches across. *She flatters him with a mischievous look at his soapy buttocks.*

MAYA

Surprise me.

He burst into song. Maya steps back and with her hands behind her she fishes inside his trousers. She locates the keys, watch and ring. She joins in enthusiastically with the song as he reaches the chorus.

He turns off the water.

Hey! Keep that on ... I'm coming in too ... I want that body covered in soap and I'll check out your bubbles!

COYOTE 2
(turning on the shower again)

Yihoooooo!

He bursts into another well-known song as he plasters on the soap. She steps out into the room and sticks the key in the lock.

What a voice! What a body!

She unlocks the door and opens it gently.

MAYA
(quietly)

What a prick.

As a last thought she picks up his boots.

COYOTE 2

Come on, baby ... I'm all soaped up and ready to scrub!

The noisy flow of water stops. There is another click as Maya locks the door from outside.

His triumphant grin pokes round the corner. He rushes into the room covered in soap with his hands round his bollocks. He pulls at the door but it is locked.

> (*banging the door*)
> Open the fucking door! Open the doooor!

He heaves at the handle. It comes off in his hand and he nearly slips.

> Bastard!

He moves to the open window. He catches sight of Maya sprinting along the street.

> *Madre de la gran chingada!* [Mother of the great fucker!]
> Come back here!

Maya turns round briefly, to see his soapy image at the window. She holds up his boots to taunt him.

> My boots! No! No! My new fucking boots!

Maya runs off into the crowd.

Sprawling shops spilling out to the street. Maya's image flashes between cars speeding past. Maya deals with a trader standing in front of his shoeshop. She hands over the Coyote's boots for a quick sale.

JOURNEY TO ROSA'S HOUSE

Maya sits in the back of a taxi. She passes Crocket Street and is momentarily stunned. Hundreds of homeless, like some refugee camp.

The taxi turns a corner and she stares up Fifth Street to the surreal shimmer of glass office blocks.

Taxi heads in the direction of MacArthur Park. All along the pavement rows of men and women sell everything and anything. There are no stalls, everything is simply laid out on the concrete, from old clothes to battered electronics, second-hand tools, nuts, screws and car parts – the bottom end of the flea market. Every sign is in Spanish, every face Latino.

The taxi turns into a side street in which kids play football. Faces peer from windows.

The taxi pulls up outside an old decaying merchant house with a veranda, now under multiple occupancy. Maya jumps out and the taxi speeds off.

By the front door she sees Luis (eight years old) playing with a toy truck.

MAYA

Luis! *Como estas?* It's me ... Maya. How you doing?

LUIS

Maya! Mama! Maya's here!

He rushes towards her. Maya swings him round.

MAYA

You're so big!

Sudden scream as Simona (sixteen) runs towards her and they embrace.

SIMONA

Maya! Maya! What happened? Mama got such a fright! Oh, man!

MAYA

Look at you! You're nearly taller than me!

Bert (fifties, white and English-speaking) and Rosa rush towards her.

BERT

Hey, skinny! Come here!

All three tangle up together.

ROSA
(*hugging her tight*)
Thanks be to God you're OK. Thanks be to God!

> (*pause*)

You must be starving.

ROSA'S HOUSE. KITCHEN

Almost tenderly, Rosa savours photographs brought by Maya.
Simona and Luis crowd round. Maya devours her meal.

> ROSA
> (*photograph of her mother*)

Look at her hair ... it's all combed up ... She's got her best
dress on ...

> SIMONA

We sent that for Grandma's birthday.

> ROSA
> (*another photograph*)

She's skin and bone ... Look at her little arms.

> BERT

Pass 'em over.

Rosa flicks through some more. Luis calls out their names as Maya
interjects with news.

> LUIS

Grandma and Uncle Pedro [Maya's older brother] ...

> MAYA

Got a job as a teacher.

> LUIS

Martha ...

> MAYA

Madly in love.

> LUIS

Who's that?

ROSA

Natalia, *corazon* ... my cousin ...

MAYA

Who's had another two babies since you seen her last ...

SIMONA

Helena, your second cousin?

Rosa nods.

Who lives next door ...

MAYA

Not any more ... She ran off with a policeman!

ROSA

Sour-faced bitch ... Serves her right.

SIMONA

Mama!

Photographs of a few children.

ROSA

Look at the size of them! *Que guapos todos!*

Next a photograph of Maya and the two youngest, at nineteen and fifteen.

LUIS

Maya, Daniel and Eva ...
                    (*to Maya*)
I think you're the prettiest.

Laughter.

MAYA

I think you're gorgeous too!

The last photograph: Claudia, second oldest after Rosa, poses, like some star in a tele-novella, blowing a kiss. More laughter.

That's for you, Bert. There's a message on the back.

He grabs it and sounds out the words in clumsy Spanish.

BERT
'*Un besote en la calva . . .*'

SIMONA
'A kiss on your baldy head . . .'

BERT
'*Te casaste con la hermana incorrecta!*'

SIMONA
'You married the wrong sister!'

Laughter.

BERT
You're telling me!

Maya wipes up the last of the sauce with a tortilla.

ROSA
Right, you two . . . Homework. Now!

Simona and Luis clear out. Maya pulls Rosa's watch and wedding ring from her pocket and slides them across to Rosa. Rosa stares at her ring in disbelief.

My God . . . You got it back.

She examines her ring and then puts it on.

I knew you'd manage.

MAYA
(*Spanish*)
Jesus Christ, Rosa! They could have raped me . . . Anything could have happened! What the hell were you playing at?

ROSA
(*Spanish*)

I don't have a cent since Bert got sick ... That's the truth ...
We're up to there.

MAYA
(*Spanish*)

I know that! But you said you were organized ... Why the hell
didn't you say?

ROSA
(*Spanish*)

I did say! You push too hard, Maya! You always do! And
never listen ... Jesus ... Everything was done in a rush!

Bert looks perturbed.

BERT

Rosa ... easy. What is it?

MAYA
(*English*)

You said you had it fixed up ... You don't mess with these
guys ... What happened?

ROSA

I know someone who runs a bar ... I got you a job there ...
He promised me $800 as an advance on your wages ... A big
favour, believe me ... I know him from way back ... It was all
organized and that's what I told you on the phone ... But he
didn't tell his brother ... They had an argument ... When I
went round this morning he gave me only $300.

Long silence.

MAYA

I want a cleaning job with you at the office block.

ROSA

So do hundreds of others ... We've been through this before ...

MAYA

I'm fitter! Faster...

ROSA

Maya! I've asked the supervisor a dozen times! Please!

Pause.

MAYA

What kind of bar is it?

ROSA

What do you mean 'what kind of bar'?

MAYA

What kind of bar?

ROSA

It ain't a cocktail lounge in Beverly Hills if that's what you mean!

MAYA

I don't want to work in a bar like that.

ROSA

Puta madre! Don't get me angry on your first night ... Why the hell couldn't you wait six months ... give me time?

MAYA

Cause I got fired, that's how!

ROSA

And why did you get fired? Because you can't keep it shut ... It was a great job ... right close to Mama ... You should never have left her.

MAYA

Rosa ... drop it!

ROSA

You're a dreamer sometimes ... You don't know what it's like up here.

MAYA

I'm going to pay you back. Every cent.

ROSA

That's not what I meant!

Luis appears at the door holding a book.

LUIS

Maya, can you read me a story?

BAR. NIGHT

A couple of 'hostesses' deliver drinks back and forth. Seedy dance floor, with a hideous blonde nymph lying backwards over a rock painted on the far wall. Other hostesses on the dance floor are clutched in groping embraces by men of mixed ages, most with sizeable pot-bellies.

Maya, virtually unrecognizable in a tiny miniskirt with sequins and a scanty top, puts several drinks on a table. A boozy customer tries to stick the money in her pants.

The music changes to a sparky recodo. *A tubby customer lets out a yell and drags Maya to the dance floor as he attempts a hilarious* quebradita (*a dance with lots of jumping, twisting, kicking and throwing the partner in the air*). *Maya isn't amused as she is clumsily tossed into the rafters.*

SITTING ROOM/BEDROOM. NIGHT

Maya leans over her bedside table and writes a letter. The statue of the Virgin sits under the lamp. Luis and Simona are fast asleep in the same room.

The letter fades into the next scene.

MAYA
(*voice-over; Spanish*)
... It's a cocktail lounge, Mama, with a polished wooden

dance floor. Most of the customers are businessmen, with good manners, and I got $50 tip the first week, but I'd rather work with Rosa at the office blocks. Once I clear the debts I'll wire down some money, as soon as I can. Luis and Simona are great kids and study hard. Bert doesn't look so good. He's a kind man and loves Rosa . . .

STREET. DAY

Rosa and Maya work from the back of Bert's old truck, by a corner, selling jolotes (*corn*) *and home-made tacos.*

Opposite, on the other corner, twenty day labourers, all Latino, wait to be hired. Some play cards as they sit on a wall. Others stare into the distance, lost in thought.

> MAYA
> (*voice-over; Spanish*)
> . . . She looks exhausted but never complains. She cleans late shift and gets up first thing to sell tacos to the *jornaleros* who hang around street corners, waiting and waiting, hoping for a day's work. Sometimes they're lucky . . . I miss cooking with you, Mama! And all that chat, especially the dirty jokes you pick up at the bakery! People don't laugh much here . . . They're too busy. I'll write soon. Love, Maya.

Banter between Rosa, Maya and a few of the men buying food.

A van looking for workers pulls up at the far side. The men swarm round, in competition, jostling and shouting for attention. The van speeds off with three workers. The disappointed disperse once again.

A young worker waiting for food eavesdrops on Maya's conversation.

> MAYA
> (*all Spanish*)
> . . . It's a shit-hole bar . . . My feet are black and blue with the clumsy pricks jumping on my toes . . .

20

ROSA

I've worked in a bar too ...

MAYA

This is different ... Slimy perverts ...

Young worker listens more intently.

One managed to stick a $5 bill right inside my pants ... Then
it's all dirty talk ... dancing, squeezing up against me like a
scabby dog with a hard-on ... Next he tries to kiss me ... with
his tongue! ...
                          (*to young worker*)
What are you fucking smiling at, you little shrimp?
                          (*pause*)
Ask him once more, Rosa ...

ROSA

How many times have I got to tell you ...

MAYA

                          (*interrupting*)
Once more! Once more ...

ROSA

I don't own the fucking office block! I just clean there!

MAYA

Just ask him to see me.

ROSA

Do you ever listen? I've already asked!

MAYA

I've got to get out of that bar, Rosa.

*A police car pulls up on the far side of the road. Tension all round.
A couple of young workers walk off smartly.*

                          (*nervous*)
Jesus ... What do I do?

ROSA

Cool it ... It's the police ... not the Migra.

MAYA

Jesu Christo.

OFFICE BLOCK ENTRANCE. EVENING

Rosa, dressed in distinctive Angel Services overalls, and Maya walk along at speed towards the office block. Obviously they're arguing, which attracts the attention of Ernest, a well-built security guard, who peers at them through the glass façade.

They arrive at the entrance.

ROSA

You can't come in here.

MAYA

I'm not moving ... I swear I'll stay here all night.

Rosa charges through the revolving door and joins Ella (mid-thirties, African American) at the elevator.

ELLA

Are you OK, baby?

Rosa just nods. She turns to look at Maya. Her image flashes before her in between revolutions of the door. She still looks at Rosa hopefully. Maya points to the ground and indicates she's staying put as the elevator door closes.

Outside, Maya stares at the revolving doors to the entrance as if she's mesmerized. Distinctive rhythmic swishing sound.

White men in suits out. Brown women in overalls in. Around and around. A few women power-dressers and heavily made-up secretaries. A few men in overalls.

Around and around they spin, neither world meeting.

Ernest, the security guard, comes through the doors and moves towards her.

ERNEST

Hey, you! Can't stay here! Move along!

Maya ignores him.

You speak English? You hear me, girl?

MAYA

I speak English. I hear you fine.

ERNEST

Well, move it!

Ruben (Mexican, mid-twenties), dressed in the same overalls, comes over to her. He's with Juan (same age, more or less).

RUBEN

Are you OK?

ERNEST

Who's asking you? ... Get in there!

Ruben ignores him. Calm and gentle.

RUBEN

Are you OK?

ERNEST

Mind your own fucking business and do what you're told!

MAYA

I'm OK.

JUAN

Come on, man ... Let's go ...
            (*smiling at Ernest, then in Spanish*)
Big constipated fucking bandy-legged hairy asshole . . .
                    (*English*)
Ruben, listen to the man.

Maya backs off. Ruben, without being aggressive or frightened, holds Ernest's eye for a moment and all three head back in and leave Maya by herself.

Maya drifts over beside a piece of modern art in the middle of the plaza. Office towers surrounds her on four sides. She turns round and looks back up towards the top of the enormous office block, which makes her dizzy. Almost surreal. Half the dark panes of glass catch the stunning reflection of sunset and half look black as hell.

She waits.

Rosa comes through the revolving doors and lets out a whistle. Maya sprints over to her.

> MAYA
>
> I knew you could do it!

Rosa is stone cold.

JANITORS' ROOM

Maya stands opposite the cleaning supervisor, Mr Perez (forties, Latino, but second generation with poor Spanish, handsome in a rough sort of way), in his little office, which is cordoned off by glass in the corner of the cleaners' canteen. Canteen has a place for clocking in at the entrance, lockers, tables and chairs. Both Maya and Perez are visible to the curious cleaners getting ready for the shift.

> MAYA
> (*all English*)
> Thanks for this chance, Mr Perez. I'll work hard.

> PEREZ
>
> I know you will ... It's about time we got rid of some of these old fuckers anyways ...
> (*examining her uniform*)
> It's just slightly loose.

He pinches the uniform above her shoulder and lifts it up a little and down again. It's an excuse to tighten the fabric against her breasts.

That's better ...

Maya shyly squirms from him. He catches several of the women, including Berta and Dolores, watching him. He sits down.

Do you know, I get begging letters to work here ... You're lucky, know that?

He pauses, waiting for an answer. Maya acknowledges what he says with a slight nod.

Yes, you are ... I do Rosa a special favour... I like Rosa ... arrange the paperwork, decent paperwork, not the shit you get at MacArthur Park ... at great personal risk, so ... I charge commission.

MAYA

What kind of commission?

PEREZ

Your first month's salary ...

The colour drains from Maya's face.

We can split it over two months ... What do you say?

Maya looks to the ground and then out at Rosa and Ella, who stare in at her.

That uniform might fit someone else a little better ...

MAYA

OK.

In one corner of the canteen Marina, a tough woman from Russia, stands on a stool, calls out the names (including Olga, Dolores, Berta, Anna, Teresa, Ella) and throws out different sets of keys from hooks on the wall inside a cupboard. She does so swapping between English and pigeon Spanish, all with her own heavy Russian accent.

Ruben, Juan and Ben (Salvadorian, older, natural authority and thoughtful) sit on the bench beside Rosa, while Marina continues to distribute the keys.

All three men have their eye on Maya. Juan, sitting beside Rosa, drools the most.

> JUAN
> (*Spanish*)
> Fuck ... she's hot! Cute little ass ... Get my hands on that! Bet she does tricks! ...
> > (*he turns to Rosa*)
> Rosa ... who is she?

> ROSA
> My sister.

ANOTHER CORRIDOR

Maya, soaked in sweat, confronts a huge expanse of carpet. She battles with an enormous vacuum cleaner in jerky frenetic movements (up five metres, back five metres).

Ella studies the comic situation with some sympathy. She marches up behind Maya and taps her on the shoulder. Maya jumps with fright and turns off the machine.

Hearty laugh from Ella.

> ELLA
> This ain't the Olympic Games, baby ... You training for a marathon?

She wipes Maya's brow with a hanky.

> MAYA
> I'll never finish on time ...

ELLA

You gonna give yourself a heart condition ...
(demonstrating movements with the machine but without turning it on)
You gotta loosen up, relax those muscles ... or after midnight you're a zombie! ... Get into a rhythm, swing those shoulders, swing those hips, or your arms seize up and you got a stiff neck for a week ...

She almost swoons with tremendous rhythm. Maya laughs easily.

Pretend you're dancing, block out the noise ... and time sails by ...
(back to earth)
The secret is ... keep the muscles loose, into a rhythm ... and never ever go back to unplug it ...
(with a flick of her wrist, she snaps at the flex – thirty-five metres away the plug comes free and she begins to wind the flex round her shoulder)
... or you never finish in time ... It's like cleaning twenty houses, baby ... so pace yourself.

MAYA

Thanks, Ella ...
(examining her hand)
It's harder than it looks.

ELLA

How come you speak good English?

MAYA

It's a long story ... My aunt worked for gringos ... cleaning, cooking, looking after their kids ... I was the same age ... grew up with them.

Ella plugs the machine in again at a power point right beside them. Maya switches on the vacuum and tries to copy Ella.

Hope you do salsa better, baby!

BY THE ELEVATOR DOORS

Maya and Ruben (wearing a mask) kneel down between elevator doors and polish the tracks of the elevator (a golden-coloured chrome on the base of the elevator which passengers step over and on once it stops at a floor). She can't help but notice his big brown eyes.

RUBEN
(*Spanish*)
Use a screwdriver like this ...
(*he has a screwdriver inside a cloth to peel the dust and dirt from a ridged track*)
or you'll never finish in time ...

The released dust blows up into Maya's face.

Sorry ... the wind blows the shit up into your face ... Need to buy yourself a mask ... Take this one.

MAYA
No!

RUBEN
Yeah!

He puts it on her.

Two men emerge from an office and squeeze between and almost over Ruben and Maya and into the elevator.

You want to hear my theory about ...
(*indicating his*)
overalls?
(*pause*)
They make white men blind!

Maya looks up into the elevator. They just don't see her. They press the button and disappear. Maya laughs at Ruben's 'See what I mean?' look.

They hear more executives around a corner. Suddenly Maya dives into the other elevator just by the side of the one which has disappeared.

MAYA
(great urgency, whispered)
Hold the door! Quick!

Ruben holds the door of the elevator and watches in amazement as Maya presses dozens of buttons for different floors.

RUBEN
Jesus Christ, woman! What you doing?

She dives out again. Ruben grabs her hand and they sprint into an adjoining office just as three executives turn the corner. One of them rushes to the elevator door and holds it open for the others to enter.

EXECUTIVE
(triumphantly)
Made it!

Ruben and Maya peek around the office door.

EXECUTIVES
(sudden, as the elevator door closes)
What the hell! ... Twenty fucking floors!

Maya is delighted. Ruben smiles with her.

RUBEN
You're crazy!

BUS. TWO-THIRTY A.M.

The bus is predominantly full of cleaners. Ruben and Juan sit opposite Maya.

Other faces look drained and exhausted. Juan nods off and his head falls on to Ruben's shoulder. Maya smiles at him.

An older woman puts some cream on her leathery hands.

BEDROOM. NIGHT

Maya writes at her desk while Simona and Luis sleep soundly.

> MAYA
> (voice-over; Spanish)
> ... It sounds silly, Mama, but coming back in the bus tonight it's like I see you everywhere ... Folks dropping off to sleep and snoring! Just like you do! We got Mexicans, Salvadorians, Nicas, Hondurans ... Lots more came up since Hurricane Mitch, Indians from Guatemala ... We're all here ... It's a strange atmosphere at night-time ... just us, no white people ... Sometimes I daydream and think I'm back home ...
> (thinking for a moment, and fidgeting with the statue of the Virgin of Guadalupe)
> Meal-times ... that's when I miss you most ... I was feeling sorry for myself last week till I spoke to Rosa's neighbour ... She hasn't seen her kids for ten years. Ten years! She shows me every new photograph she gets ... all lined up on her wall. I nearly cried the first time. Now I just get mad ... It's not right, Mama ...

She scribbles a farewell, folds up the letter and puts it in an envelope.

FADE.

THE OFFICES. A CORRIDOR

Maya is by herself and working hard. She sticks her mop into a bucket of wax and skims it on like an expert.

Suddenly she hears distant footsteps. They stop. Now a little louder. They disappear again.

She works on, getting closer to a crossroads of swing doors. She gets back into the rhythm. Again some steps that she can't quite place.

The swing doors burst open with an almighty crash. Sam (late twenties, attractive but unkempt), wearing a bright red T-shirt, sprints towards her. She panics and squeezes up against the wall.

SAM

Is that wax?

She nods. He picks it up and hurls it along the corridor.

Sorry.

He sprints off again. Again another crash as both swing doors open simultaneously and two burly security guards, Ernest and Freddy, from the reception storm through. They both hit the wax and immediately skid on to their asses and come flying towards Maya. Another crash and Perez steams through and hits the wax as well. He skids on his feet, just maintaining balance till he trips over a security guard.

They all curse like mad.

ERNEST

Where'd the fucker go?

Maya hesitates and then points down the corridor. All three disappear. Maya stares at the mess. She catches her breath.

Sam pops his head around the corner from a room off the corridor. He tiptoes carefully round the mess and peers through a window on the swing door he's just come through. He catches sight of another security guard with a walkie-talkie.

He turns to Maya, who is still half stunned against the wall.

SAM

I'm real sorry about the mess ...

He hears the noise of returning footsteps.

34

Shit ... I can explain everything ...

There is a certain boyish charm as he holds her eye – mischief, but no fear.

No soy ladron ...
>   (*in response to her doubt*)
> te prometo ... Don't turn me in ...

Maya can't believe her eyes as he jumps into the enormous bin in the middle of her service trolley. (The service trolley has places for cleaning materials front and back. In the middle is a big bin. The whole thing is pushed along on a trolley.)

Just get me to the service elevator at the end of the corridor ...
>   (*in response to her shock*)
It'll take just thirty seconds and I'll be gone.

He disappears just as the trio burst through the doors again. They are furious. All three carry walkie-talkies. Perez limps. They stand beside Maya.

> ERNEST

We lost him.

> CONTROL

Assholes ... Fucking assholes!

> FREDDY

Will you stop calling us that!

> CONTROL

Give me one good reason, asshole!

> PEREZ

My fucking leg ...

> ERNEST
> (*limping too*)

I'll kill the bastard!

Perez grabs some paper towels from Maya's trolley and begins to wipe the wax from his trousers. Freddy does the same. Maya stares at them, dumbfounded. Perez is about to stick towels in the bin but Maya takes them from him.

> MAYA
> (*wiping*)

You missed some . . .

She takes the towel from Freddy too.

> PEREZ
> (*into walkie-talkie*)

Block every exit . . . every mouse-hole . . . We've got the bastard this time!
> (*punching the top of the trolley*)

Let's move it!

Maya starts to push the trolley off and struggles with its weight.

> FREDDY

You too pretty for this job. What you got in there?

Maya freezes.

> MAYA

Books . . . old telephone books.

She passes through the swing doors and again along the corridor.

> SAM
> (*poking up the lid*)

Thanks! How you doing?

> MAYA

Get down and shut up!

> SAM

You're new here . . . What's your name?

He lifts up the lid a little more to shed some light on a list he has on his hand.

Berta? Rosa? Teresa? *Definitely* not Juan …

MAYA

Get down!

SAM

Anna?

MAYA

Where you get that list?

Ernest comes sprinting through the doors.

SAM

CIA.

Maya smashes the lid down on his head. Groan from inside. Ernest runs past. Sam pops his head up again, but Maya smacks it back down again.

They reach the service elevator.

MAYA

Right, asshole … out of here!

Sam jumps out and skips into the elevator.

SAM
(*indicating the list*)
It was on the notice-board …

MAYA

Who the hell are you?

Shouts from the guards approaching. He presses the button.

SAM
(*glancing at list*)
Maya! Lovely hands!

The doors close shut.

ROSA'S HOUSE

Sam walks up the street, checking the numbers. He knocks on a door. Rosa answers.

SAM

Sam Shapiro, Justice for Janitors campaign ...

ROSA

Rosa, Justice for Rosa campaign. What you want?

Bert appears at the door with Maya, really surprised, behind him.

BERT

Who is it?

MAYA

He's come to throw wax all over the floor.

SAM

Maya!

BERT

You know him? What you selling?

SAM

Do you mind if I come in for a few minutes?

BERT

We don't need no wax.

MAYA

And then he'll dive into the trash can.

Sam laughs.

ROSA

Ha! This the joker you told me about?

Bert stares at him suspiciously.

SAM

I'm working with the janitors' union.

MAYA

Come in.

SAM

Ahh ... She your sister?

Maya nods.

MAYA

Rosa ... and her husband, Bert.

SAM

You saved my ass ... Thanks a lot.

Sam enters the crammed sitting room. The scissors beds are up against the wall. Rosa fusses round, picking up clothes. Simona and Luis do homework on the dining table.

BERT

Suppose ya want money?

SAM

More money than you've ever imagined ...

Sam hesitates for a moment, then takes something from his pocket and holds it out to Bert.

Look at that. Know what it is?

Bert hesitates, still suspicious. Simona takes it.

SIMONA

A wage slip.

SAM

How much per hour?

SIMONA

$8.50.

SAM

Date?

SIMONA

22 December 1982 ... It's a Capricorn wage slip.

SAM

Seventeen years ago ... seventeen! ... that cleaner earned $8.50 ... plus health, plus sick pay, plus holidays ... Today ... Los Angeles, 1999, if you don't have a union deal you only get $5.75 ... plus nothing!

Maya takes the wage slip and examines it.

We've worked it out ... Over the last twenty years billions of dollars have been sucked out of the poorest communities in this city ... It went from your homes into their banks ... And you know what? ... We're going to get it back. Not millions ... but billions! I mean it ...
> (*to Simona*)

You think I'm mad, think I'm joking?

SIMONA

I think you're cute. What's your star sign?

They all laugh easily bar Bert and Rosa.

BERT

You and whose army, Mister?

Rosa at last sits down.

SAM

Does Rosa ever work late?

BERT

No ... she's too busy playing golf.

SAM

Does she get overtime?

BERT

Are you on the run from some asylum?

Health care? Dental care? Not just for her but the whole family? How many years you been cleaning, Rosa?

She doesn't respond.

SIMONA

Ten years ...

SAM

If you had a union contract ... you'd get four weeks' holidays
...
(*to Bert*)
How many jobs you got?

Silence. Maya watches him carefully.

Can you survive on one job? $5.75 an hour?

SIMONA

$240 a week.

SAM

Exactly! With a family? No way! ... Everybody's working two jobs ... maybe three ...
(*glancing at Simona and Luis*)
Kids left alone ...

SIMONA

Orphans ... that's what we are ... Why don't you come baby-sit?

Maya really laughs, which just encourages them.

BERT

Cool it.

SIMONA

Abandoned ... disturbed ... Look ... he's got a tic, I joined a gang ...

Luis obliges and hams it up.

43

BERT

Cut it out!

SIMONA

No time to bond! Mama, listen to this guy ... We want three weeks' holiday in the Caribbean ...

Sam and Maya, glancing at each other and Simona, think this is very funny. Bert doesn't.

SAM

What happens if one of the kids gets ill ... or Rosa?

Silence for a moment.

LUIS

Papa's sick.

Silence.

SAM

I'm sorry ... I didn't realize.

SIMONA

He needs an operation ... If he doesn't get an operation soon ... he'll get worse, much worse.

Silence. Bert stares at the floor in embarrassment.

SAM

What's wrong?

MAYA

Diabetic ... His eyes are playing up ...

BERT

That's my problem!

SAM

Bull-shit!

Maya is shocked.

44

You're ill, she's probably working sixteen hours a day ... the kids lose out ... all because those bastards at Angel won't pay health insurance! How much the sugar-kits cost? $250 ... $300?

> SIMONA

And he's run out of test strips.

Maya notices Sam's flushed cheeks.

> MAYA

If Rosa had health care ... you'd be treated by now.

> ROSA

'If!' If, if ... If I hear that word once more!

> SAM

It doesn't have to be 'if' ... Union buildings downtown, janitors have health care ... every one of them! ... But don't take my word for it ... Speak to workers there themselves ... Would you speak to them, Rosa?
> (*long pause*)
> If you could just get a few of the cleaners together, they'll tell you how they did it ... step by step.

> BERT

If the company hears about this ... they're out ...

> SAM

Start with a few you can trust ...

> ROSA

I trust nobody ...

> SAM

... in a safe place ...

> ROSA

One mistake and I'm on black-list! You any idea what those *pendejos* are like?

SIMONA

Mama!

SAM

There's every chance ...

ROSA

There's every chance you'll get fired! I've seen it before, so
don't give me *tonterias* ... Are you going to pay the rent ...
feed my kids?

Sam looks at Maya.

(*to Maya*)
You keep away from this, *payaso*!

MAYA

They'll fire you anyways ... one word out of place ... the
wrong look ...

ROSA

(*real venom*)
Listen to the expert after three months! ... You've always got
the answers ... always ... till you fuck up another job ... But
I'll get you another one ...
(*snapping her fingers*)
Just like that! Easy!

SIMONA

Grovelling gets you nowhere.

BERT

Simona!

Bert stares at his daughter and then at Sam.

ROSA

Right ...
(*to the kids*)
Homework, you two ...

(*dismissing Sam*)

That's it ... We're busy ... We might be at the bottom of the shit-hole, but we're doing our best.

SAM

(*sharp*)

And that's where we'll stay if we let them get away with it.

ROSA

(*frightening*)

'We' ... We! ... When was the last time you had a cleaning job? ... You and your union ... Fat union white boys ... College kids ... What the hell you know?

SIMONA

Mama ... *tranquila*!

SAM

This campaign is different ...

ROSA

Don't ever say 'we' ... I believe in NOTHING! NOBODY! NEVER! Do you hear me? Nothing but that!

She holds up her hand.

SAM

Listening never hurt anyone, Rosa ... That's all I'm asking ...

ROSA

We don't need no lessons about *our life* ... hear me, wise guy? Right, get out.

Deadly silence.

SAM

Thanks for your time.

Sam heads for the door.

STREET OUTSIDE ROSA'S HOUSE

Sam begins to head down the street.

MAYA

Sam.

He turns round. Maya holds out a cold drink. Sam smiles and gratefully takes a long sup.

How many houses you been to?

SAM
(*hesitation*)

Six.

MAYA

How you get on?

Sam gives the thumbs-down.

You forgot something.

Maya hands him the wage slip.

Was that a real wage slip?

SAM

Yip.

Emma, another union activist, whistles to him from further down the street and indicates he should get a move on.

MAYA

So you're going to change the world?

Sam studies her for a moment and hands her back the glass.

SAM

If Bert had health insurance would that make a difference?

MAYA

Suppose so.

SAM

What about that multiplied by the 10,000 non-union cleaners in this city?

(*pause*)

Then their families?

Emma whistles again.

MAYA

Think she likes you.

There is a moment between them. Sam hands her his card.

He heads off to join Emma. Maya watches him leave. He glances round at her before joining Emma.

OFFICE BLOCK. EVENING

Revolving doors. White out. Brown in.

CANTEEN. EVENING

The clock shows a couple of minutes to seven p.m. Some cleaners still clock in, others pick up their keys and others sit round different tables. Some stare into space by themselves. Ruben sits between Maya and Juan.

Ruben has several books open in front of him and he copies out the last of some notes. Juan has obviously been bugging him with questions for some time, which causes amusement to the other listeners. Maya tries not to laugh.

JUAN
(*all Spanish*)
... One book, then another book, another book ...
(*to Maya*)
Three years he's been doing this ... Comes in early! ... How many books you gonna read? Eh? ... And you know what gets me ... Look ... He's copying there ...

(sticking a tapping finger right into his notebook)
what's already . . .
(stabbing a finger)
in there . . . What's the fucking point of that, eh? Supposed to
be smart . . . Ha! . . . Know what I keep asking myself?
(pause, then triumphantly)
Why don't you just fucking photocopy it!

This sends Maya into giggles, which only encourages him.

(elbowing him)
What you gonna be anyways?

ROSA

A brain surgeon. Know what he's going to do then? Get a big
microscope this size . . . Going to try and locate your fucking
pea-sized brain . . . and get your IQ up to the standard of an
average monkey . . . And if he can do that . . . he'll win a Nobel
Prize for his contribution to my sanity!

JUAN

You saw that movie . . .

ROSA
(pulling his cap right down over his face)
Shut it!

*Maya browses through one of Ruben's books. She helps him
gather them together as they get up to start their shift.*

*Two older Latina woman rush in and move to the clocking-in
device. Both sweat profusely. Anna sticks her card in just as the
second hand goes by the hour. The other woman, Teresa (fifties),
fumbles with hers and drops it on the ground. Anna picks it up for
her and is about to stick it in when Perez grabs it from her hand.*

He walks to the middle of the room.

PEREZ
Come here! What time does it say up there?

51

Marina (*dishing out keys in the corner*) *and all the others go quiet as Teresa, humiliated, joins him as requested.*

What time does it say up there?

Teresa looks to the ground.

Are you deaf? The time ... the exact time ... what's it say? Oh ... can't tell the time!

> TERESA
> (*whisper*)

I can't see the clock ...

> PEREZ

What? Can't hear you!

> TERESA

I can't see the clock.

She still looks to the ground. Maya, furious, can't help herself and starts to move forward. Rosa grabs her.

> ROSA
> (*whispering*)

Don't start!

> PEREZ
> (*realizing she hasn't got glasses*)

Ahhh ... now we know ...

Maya shakes Rosa free but is beaten to it by Ella.

> ELLA
> (*barely controlled fury*)

It's seven o'clock and thirty seconds ... thirty God-damned seconds!

Perez looks round furiously at her but she holds his eye.

ROSA
(*whispering*)
Cool it ... cool it. Think of your kids.

ANNA
(*to Perez*)
Please, Mr Perez ... the bus was late ... We ran ... as fast as
we could.

PEREZ
(*to Teresa*)
Right ... you lose a shift ... and don't come back here
without glasses ... Geriatrics and now the blind ... Bring in
the cripples! ... The lepers! ... It's a fucking business, not a
holiday camp for spastics!

ANNA
(*to Teresa, walking away*)
Teresa!

PEREZ
Do yourself a favour ... Don't come back at all! You can
never finish in time ... Find something else, for Christ sake.

MAYA
(*under her breath*)
Bastard ... bastard!

ANNA
Please, Mr Perez ...

PEREZ
You want to take a walk too? Give you lot an inch ... you
take a mile ... Jesus Christ!

*Teresa, totally humiliated, quietly leaves and shushes Anna away
with a few gentle whispers.*

Maya stares at Perez from the corner. Ruben stands beside her.

RUBEN
(*quietly to Maya, as Teresa disappears*)
She looks like my mother.

Maya fumes.

TOILET

Anna fights to control herself. Rosa comforts her. Ella, Maya and Cynthia, another cleaner, quietly watch on.

ANNA
I'm sorry ... I'm sorry ...

ROSA
Easy, easy ...

ANNA
What's she going to do? It's nothing to do with being late ... We're just too slow ... He gave us another half-floor each ... I'm not even taking my breaks.

CYNTHIA
We'll help you ... take turns ... I'll speak to some of the young ones ...

MAYA
Sure I can.

ELLA
Ruben ... he's fast ... he'll help too.

ANNA
I need this job ... I send half the money home ... Teresa's the same ... We came together ... We haven't seen our family in five years.

She begins to cry. Rosa hugs her tightly till she calms down.

I'm sorry ...

ROSA

You're OK ... OK. We're going to take care of you.

ELLA

He's getting worse ... the son of a bitch ...

ANNA

I'm next. I know I am.

PHONE BOX. STREET

A street full of life and colour. Maya sticks a quarter in a public telephone box.

MAYA

I want to speak to Sam Shapiro please.

She's put through.

SAM

Sam here.

MAYA

It's Maya ... remember me?

SAM

The Toluca Street Gang! How's Bert doing?

MAYA

Just the same. Listen, something happened at work ... I want to see you.

SAM

No problem ... What's easiest?

BASEMENT ROOM

Enormous boilers and pipes. Sam and Emma stand in front of the cleaners. Some are eating. Juan chews on an enormous burrito. A grim-faced Marina and Olga stare in silence. Rosa stands by Maya. Ben keeps watch at the door.

SAM

This is maybe the most important building in the city right now ... Why? Angel Services are one of the biggest cleaning companies in the country ... They've targeted prestige offices and have successfully bid against union cleaning companies ...

EMMA

They don't pay health insurance, sick pay ... holidays, nothing ... It saves them $300 per worker per month ... which means they can undercut everybody. Cleaners, like you, pay the price ... If they are seen to get away with it ... we'll lose everything we've fought for over the last ten years ...

SAM

Other sharks will move in, just like that!

OSCAR (CLEANER)

But even if we force Angel to unionize ... what's to stop the owners of the building dumping Angel at the end of the month?

MARINA

Pick up another non-union company for Christ sake ... just like they dumped the last one!

OSCAR

Then we're all out of a job ... and you're back to square one!

MARINA

Exactly!

EMMA

Correct! No point just fighting *your* company ... Angel Services ...

Sam unrolls a flyer he has, turns it over and beckons Ben to hold it against a wall for him. He starts drawing on it with a marker as he speaks.

SAM

Take any building ...

    (drawing one in the middle of the flyer)

here we got the OWNERS ...

    (drawing smaller and circled)

Next we got the CLEANING CONTRACTORS, Angel, next we got the TENANTS ... Now, this is where it gets interesting ... Who are the tenants here? ... Hollywood lawyers, finance houses, some of the biggest banks in the country ... These guys, big reputations, want a quiet life ... They don't want hassle from ...

    (drawing and circling)

MEDIA, CITY GOVERNMENT and COMMUNITY ...

EMMA

    (indicating)

The secret is to hassle these big-time ...

    (pointing)

TENANTS to put pressure on the OWNERS ...

SAM

We gotta force them to pick union cleaning companies ... They got the power ...

JUAN

    (Spanish)

I don't understand a fucking word ... I'm all mixed up!

MAYA

    (Spanish)

I'll tell you later.

EMMA

But ...

    (pointing to them all)

they all benefit from your cheap labour ... They all gotta feel the consequences ... Pay the price!

BEN

How do you do that?

SAM

We take it step by step ... from targeting key individuals who call the shots ...
(*pointing to the diagram*)
like the chief executive of the owners of this building, to carefully planned community action on the streets ...

CYNTHIA

What's that mean?

SAM

Imagine we block one set of traffic lights downtown at rush hour ... Imagine how many banks and corporations affected ... secretaries and lawyers tied up ... Multiply that through the city ... It's cheaper to pay you a decent wage ...

MARINA

Are you crazy? Who's gonna do that?

SAM

We've done it before ... It works.

EMMA

We've got a core of worker volunteers, students, churches, family, friends, grass-root organizers ... not just cleaners.

MARINA

Don't listen to these people ... Please don't listen.

SAM

Correct! Come and speak to the other cleaners ...

MARINA

I've seen this all my life in Russia ... Tomorrow is always better, tomorrow is always brighter, more sacrifice, more sacrifice ... But tomorrow is *never* better ... They're full of bull-shit dreams ...

MAYA

Marina, what's wrong with talking to other cleaners?

MARINA

Listen ... I'm a worker, just like you ... I've been here just
eleven months ... My English is bad, just like you ... In
Russia I got nothing, just like you ... But here I got a job ... I
feed my kids, I pay my rent ... Maybe next year I get a better
job ... Save more money, step by step ... But if you listen to
him ... just troubles ... You lose job, we lose job ... he
doesn't lose job ...

MAYA

Teresa lost her job for nothing ... Who's next?

MARINA

Maybe you're next ...

MAYA

Marina ... please let them finish ...

MARINA

Now the troubles start ... I know ...
(to *Sam and Emma*)
Please go ... Get out of our building ... We had no fights
before you came ...

MAYA

We invited them here because of Teresa.

MARINA

You invited them here ... Please go ...

MAYA

No, Marina ... We want to listen ...

ROSA
(*in Spanish*)

Cool it ...

MARINA

Shut up, please ... please ...

MAYA

You're not the boss ... You're a cleaner like the rest of us!

MARINA

Shut up ...

(*to Sam and Emma*)

Please go ...

MAYA

No, I won't shut up ... You shut up!

Rosa grabs Maya.

ROSA

(*Spanish*)

You've always got to have the last word. Shut it.

It takes Maya aback.

VOICES

Cool it ... Easy ... Keep the noise down ... Keep it down ...

Voices calm as Maya and Marina stare across at each other.

SAM

Cool it, guys ... Cool it ... Just one question before we wrap
... Why are we in the basement?

CYNTHIA

We're scared, that's why.

SAM

Exactly! Do you think that's right? No overtime, no health
care, no holidays ...

ELLA

No respect!

SAM

Do you think that's right? Nobody's forcing anybody to do anything. Just come and speak to other workers. Think about it.

Marina and Olga march out.

LAUNDRY. DAY

Rosa and Maya finish off folding up bedsheets together. Rosa avoids Maya's eye as they step in close for the final fold.

They throw the last of the next batch into a dryer and then sit down opposite each other on wooden benches. Rosa, exhausted, leans her head back. They sit quietly for a moment.

MAYA
(*all Spanish*)

Rosa ...
(*pause*)
Do you want me to leave the house?

ROSA

What the hell you talking about, girl?

MAYA

I'm not your baby sister any more ...
(*pause*)
Sometimes ... sometimes I feel you can't bear the sight of me.

After a long moment Rosa leans her head back on the wall and closes her eyes.

FADE.

STREET. DAY

An old motorbike spewing fumes and making a terrible noise turns a corner. Maya's hair blows free as she clutches Ruben's waist.

RUBEN

(*all Spanish*)

Stick out your left hand . . .

MAYA

What?

RUBEN

Left hand! The indicators don't work.

MAYA

What's going on?

RUBEN

Just wait!

They pass through the entrance gate to a college campus.

CAMPUS STEPS

Maya sits on the steps. An elated Ruben runs from the building to join her. Their cleaning uniforms are incongruous among the students. Ruben holds out a distinctive pink receipt. Maya examines it.

MAYA

You paid $1,600!

RUBEN

Been saving for ages! I'm going to college, Maya!

Maya hugs him.

I pay 20 per cent . . . they pay 80 per cent . . . It's worth over sixteen grand! Sixteen! From the moment I arrived . . . I've been dreaming about this day!

MAYA

How did you do it?

RUBEN

I did the exam! My oral was weak . . . but I was top in maths!

But I still couldn't get a scholarship ... I'm not a citizen ...
Then it was pure luck ... I found this private foundation set
up by two rich brothers ... Mexican businessmen ... They got
over 800 applicants ... and guess who they picked! Numero
uno, baby! They want me! All I got to do is prove I paid 20
per cent college fees by first day of semester ... another
$1,600, I can just do it ... and that's it!!

*Maya laughs and kisses him affectionately. They stare out at the
students streaming by. Others sit on the grass reading books.*

That must be the library.

Some students step over them.

> MAYA
>
> Look ... still can't see us.

They both laugh.

> RUBEN
>
> Know what I want? ... I want to get through this and get a
> good job ...
> > *(pause)*
> Then I want help you do the same ... You got brains.

He puts his arm around her shoulder. He kisses her.

OFFICE BLOCK. OFFICE. ANOTHER DAY

*Maya stands on shelves to clean windows with a huge squeegee.
Water drips down on her. She stops for a second to wipe her brow.*

*She stares at the sleek black and chrome buildings around her. The
city looks stunning at sunset and it stretches for miles. In the
distance she might see the Hollywood sign. She looks down and
feels her head spin at the height.*

*She looks opposite. In another office block she can see several
women cleaning the insides of windows. Her eyes continue up the
tower. Two men cleaners talking to each other wave a cloth at her.*

They laugh and joke among themselves as they see her catch sight of them.

Next Maya wipes off a magnificent desk. She examines a family picture for a moment: husband, wife, two children and golden retriever in the gardens of a luxury home. She notices thick embossed paper with stunning letterheads (Bolger, McClure, and Co.). On impulse she sits down, takes a sheet of paper and savours its quality. She picks up a fountain pen and begins to write.

MAYA

(voice-over; Spanish)

... Mama, I just moved into my new office, but things at home are not as good. You can't get a decent servant for love nor money these days ... As for a good cook ... forget it ... Besides, I need someone to walk the dog ... so I'm sending my driver ...

(pause)

Hector ...

(she grins at her own joke)

all the way down to Mexico City to pick you up ... He has strict orders to stick you in the trunk if you cause a scene ... Must rush ... I have an important meeting in New York ...

With an exaggerated flourish, she signs off with an enormous 'Maya'.

Ella pops her head round the corner.

ELLA

Something's up. Perez wants to see us.

CANTEEN. LATER

Perez, flanked by security guards, walks up and down in front of the assembled cleaners. Maya is beside Rosa and Ella. Marina stands opposite.

Perez unrolls the crumpled-up flyer used by Sam.

PEREZ
(*examining it*)
Media! Who the fuck you think you are? The White House!
(*trying to figure out a word*)
Owner? ... Ownership! None of your fucking business! ...
Join a union, they take 20 per cent ... Join a union, they
check your papers ... Join a union ... you have immigration
... No fucking union! Right?

Maya looks across at Marina. Smug satisfaction on her face.

MAYA
(*under her breath to Rosa; Spanish*)
Look at her!

ROSA
(*Spanish*)
Cut it out!

PEREZ
If we catch one of you speaking to those sons of bitches ...
(*he tears and crumples up the flyer*)
it'll be the long walk ... Bye-bye, baby ... We got cameras
everywhere ... Now get the hell out of here!

*He hurls the paper into the corner. The cleaners walk for the exit.
A quiet but furious Maya holds her ground till Marina approaches.*

MARINA
What are you staring at?

Maya holds her eye.

MAYA
(*Spanish*)
I'm staring at your big mouth.

PEREZ
Move it! Come on!

Marina walks on. The rest stream out. As Anna walks by, Perez holds her arm.

PEREZ

Just a minute.

The room clears.

Anna ... take a seat. Three and a half floors ... tough ... I know ...
(*silence*)
Takes lots of energy ... I couldn't do it ... It's a young person's work.

ANNA

I can manage! It's OK. I'm used to it ... I really am.

PEREZ

How'd you like a holiday?

ANNA

No. No. I don't need a holiday. I'm fine. I'm fine.

PEREZ

Relax. I mean a real holiday. One week's *paid* holiday ... $12.50 an hour ... yeah, *and* health insurance ...

Anna still stands nervously.

Take a seat ... We've won some new contracts ... We're looking for people we can trust ... People we know ... I can't promise ... but I do have some influence ...
(*pause*)
They're going to need some new supervisors ... Would you like that?

ANNA

Me? A supervisor?

PEREZ

Do you think you could do it?

I don't know ... but I could try. I would do my best.

PEREZ

Good ... that's all I want to know.

Long pause. Anna smiles shyly and stands up to leave.

Just one thing more. Sit down.

She sits down again.

Who organized the meeting in the basement? Who was it,
Anna?

STREET. NIGHT

Maya gets off a bus.

SAM'S HOUSE. NIGHT

Maya walks on to a street of tidy homes and neat gardens.

*She walks to the front door and starts knocking loudly. No
answer. More loud knocking. She starts banging on a window. Still
no answer.*

*She picks up a handful of pebbles and hurls them against the
window.*

*A light goes on inside. The window opens and a strange face
appears.*

MAN

Who the fuck are you? What you want?

MAYA

Sorry, I made a mistake.

MAN

Lucky I didn't blow your head off.

Sam's head appears at the flat above.

SAM

Maya! Round the side.

Maya goes round.

MAN
(*sticking his head out of the window*)
What the hell . . . Fucking punk upstairs gotta call girl!

SAM

Fucking redneck downstairs screws his poodle! And clean that shit off the lawn, you pervert!

Sam slams the window shut and disappears.

MAN
(*leaning out more*)
Fucking punk . . . come down here and say that!

Sam lets her in.

SAM

Come in, quick . . . up the stairs.

Sam leads Maya up the stairs into his sitting room. Wooden desk and computer in a corner, offbeat lamps, walls lined with books, records and cassettes. Tastefully done. Simple furniture and lots of space.

What is it? What happened?

Tight-faced, she stares at him for a moment. She hands him a torn corner of the crumpled-up flyer thrown away by Perez. Sam unravels it. Puzzlement still on his face.

So what?

MAYA
(*furious*)
So what! You don't even remember!

Maya, it's three in the morning.

MAYA

You left it in the basement!

SAM

What are you talking about?

MAYA

You threw it into the corner! Perez found it!

Sam is still puzzled.

The supervisor!

SAM

Oh, no, no ... What happened?

MAYA

Have you any idea what it's like to have him on our back? ...
Click his fingers and you're out ... eh?

SAM

Maya ...

She snaps the paper out of his hand.

MAYA

This ...
(*indicating the paper*)
shows you don't care! Underneath you're just like the rest!

SAM

Maya ... Jesus Christ ... I made a mistake.

MAYA

But you don't pay! A big game to you ... jumping into trash
cans, invading buildings ... It's exciting, isn't it?
(*silence*)
Answer me?

                          SAM

     That's not the way I see it.

She stares at him.

                          MAYA

     Just one question.
                    (*she looks round the room*)
     What do you risk?

She stares him out.

     What do you risk?
                               (*silence*)
     How much you get paid?

                          SAM
                    (*long pause*)
     $22,250.

A moment between them.

     Maya ... what happened? Did they fire you?

                          MAYA

     No.
                         (*pause*)
     They fired Anna.

She nearly cracks.

                          SAM

     Shit shit shit!

                          MAYA

     They wanted to know who organized the meeting ... but she
     wouldn't tell them.
                         (*pause*)
     Not a word!

                          SAM

     I'm really sorry. So fucking stupid of me.

(*pause*)

I just wasn't thinking.

MAYA

She's got her family in El Salvador ...
(*nearly breaking again*)
She sends all her money home ... She was saving for her
daughter's wedding ... She hasn't seen her for five years ...

Tears come to her eyes.

SAM

Easy, easy ... We'll work something out.

Long moment between them.

You're shivering ... You want a drink?

MAYA

A strong one.

*Sam disappears to get it. Maya walks round the room and wipes
her face. She notices every detail: books, music, plants,
photographs of Sam's family. There are some lovely framed prints,
including comic cartoons, another of Chilean soldiers burning
books, one of Helda Camera – 'When I give them food, they call
me a saint. When I ask why they have no food, they call me a
communist.' But pride of place goes to the imposing features of
slave abolitionist Frederick Douglass – 'Power concedes nothing
without demand. It never did and it never will.'*

*Sam returns and hands over her drink and places the bottle of
tequila on the table. He takes the initiative to chink glasses. Maya
hesitates for a moment.*

SAM

You've every right to be angry ... I'll go see Anna first thing,
and apologize to the others.

73

MAYA

Better avoid Rosa for a few weeks ... She's ready to cut your balls off!

Laughter breaks the tension.

SAM

She's tough.

MAYA

She left home at fourteen ... Went to work in the *maquiladora* factories ... I couldn't have done it ...

SAM

In Tijuana?

MAYA

Yeah! She sent money home ... She supported the whole family.

SAM

Where are you from?

MAYA

Mexico City ... but I had to live with my aunt in Cuernavaca after my father ran off ... There were too many of us ... She works for an American ... a manager in a car plant ... The wife runs a Spanish school for gringo students ... My aunt looked after their children ...

SAM

Is that where you learned English?

MAYA

I grew up with them. Started cleaning and cooking ... then I worked in the school ... administration, phone calls ... I took on more and more ...

SAM

Sounds like not a bad job ... What brought you up here?

74

Silence. Sam waits.

MAYA

They went on holiday to Europe. I was looking after the house
...
(*hesitation*)
One Saturday afternoon a few pals came round ... and then a
few more ... and then a few more ...
(*pause*)
Somehow a party got started ... a wild party ... The music
was on, full blast!

SAM

Oh, no!

MAYA

They caught seven of us in the Jacuzzi drinking cocktails.

*Sam bursts into laughter and chokes on his drink. Maya pours
herself another. Eventually Sam catches his breath.*

Came back three days early ...

*They look across at each other for a moment. Sam's silence
encourages her to continue.*

They were nice people ... good manners, never shouted, but I
always knew my place ...
(*pause*)
Even with the kids ... when we played together as children ...
they told me what to do! ... That's what they expected ...
what my aunt expected ... That's what I did! ... But I can still
remember that sick feeling in my guts ... and I can't shake it
off ... They're not bad people ... but you should have seen his
face when he found us in *his* Jacuzzi, drinking *his* drink from
his glasses ... I don't blame him for being angry ... but it was
the *disgust* in his eyes ... *la cara de asco* ...

Long silence.

75

I wanted to kick you tonight ... punch you ... I really hated you tonight! ... Never a moment of doubt under that white skin ... I thought you were different, but you still take us for granted.

She takes another gulp. Silence. She looks round the room. Tears in her eyes. She tries to control herself.

Your room's lovely!

Sam remains quiet and holds her eye.

Sometimes I get scared everything's going to turn out wrong ... I don't know what's going to happen to me ... I don't want to end up like my mother ... like Rosa ... like everybody around me!

SAM

Easy ... easy.

MAYA

Sometimes I'm scared of everything.

Sam comes over to her. She grips on to him. He hugs her tightly.

CANTEEN

All the cleaners apart from Marina and Olga sit huddled around a table in serious conversation.

Freddy (security) talks to Perez inside the latter's office.

MAYA

Right! We've discussed it long enough ...
(*looking up at the clock, which shows a few minutes past ten p.m.*)
It's now or never!

ELLA

Now!
                    (*standing up*)
We're all going! Right now! Come on!

76

MAYA

Let's go!

They get up to leave. Freddy's face pops up at the window and he alerts Perez. Both rush to the door.

PEREZ

Where the fuck you think you're going?

Several of the cleaners hesitate. Maya marches up to Perez.

MAYA

Lunch-time's our time!

FREDDY

Says who?

Maya hands Perez several sheets of paper.

MAYA

Says the court ... Read this judgement before you do something stupid. If you don't want a half-million-dollar lawsuit on your boss's desk, you leave us alone!

Ella forces the cleaners past the stunned Perez and Freddy.

ELLA

We'll be back on time ... don't you worry.

PUBLIC SPACE

The group walk towards the meeting point. Maya runs up to Ella and takes her arm.

As they get closer they can see cleaners (with different uniforms) in small groups of twos and threes walking from every direction.

ELLA

Well ... I'll be damned!

They head to a point where there are some thirty to forty cleaners congregated in the middle. There are security guards from other buildings on the periphery too.

Groups of volunteers in red shirts distribute leaflets announcing a meeting and a Janitors' Dance. There is a tug on Maya's sleeve. She turns. Anna, in a red T-shirt, distributes leaflets. Warm greetings.

Maya catches sight of Sam in the distance. He gives her a big grin and the thumbs-up. Ruben notices.

EMMA

I want to introduce some Friends of Justice for Janitors ...
We've got students here from UCLA ...

Clapping and cheers from the students.

community volunteers ... Bus Users' union ... Father Gilbert and Pastor Jack from their churches around Pico/Union.

Emma hands Sam the microphone.

SAM

I've got real good news ... For the very first time ... we got some cleaners from building 646 ... Angel Services!

Enthusiastic applause from the other cleaners.

Come on! Come up here ... Introduce yourselves.

In a semi-panic the group are herded up to the front. Sam hands the mike to Maya, who is first in the group.

Say a few words ...

MAYA

I don't know what to say!
                    (taking the mike)
Hope you can't see my legs ... cause they're shaking! But one thing's for sure ... after seeing you all here I don't feel as scared as I used to ...

Applause.

It's taken us a long time to get here ... Good to meet you ...
Hope to see you again.

Sam winks at her and passes the mike to Rosa. She's taken off guard.

SAM

Thanks for coming, Rosa.

ROSA
(*sharply*)
I'm here for one reason only! Because they fired Anna ...
There she is, over there!

Loud cheers. She thrusts the mike towards Ben. Maya and Rosa hold each other's eye for a moment.

BEN

I feel happy tonight. Thank you. When I see students here I feel good, thank you ... When I see workers from other unions, I feel something ... When I see the churches and all of us together ... all this reminds me of something we sometimes forget ... We've always got more strength than we realize! Always! That's what I learned working with *campesinos*, students and the Christian-base communities in my own country ... But sometimes, when life hits you with a heavy blow ...
(*pause*)
or you lose someone you love ...
(*pause*)
you can become angry, frightened ... even lose hope ... I have to be honest and say this has happened to me ... so thank you ...

Long applause.

They say people don't care here in Los Angeles ... It's a lie! Don't believe them! *Some* people don't care ... but some people do! We got to make these companies realize they don't fight a union ... they fight a whole community! We got to show them we're not scared ... We got to show them we got hope!

79

More loud applause. Maya is touched. Some of the security guards have moved closer. Ben notices.

Heh! We got some new friends. Give them a wave!

Amidst cheers and laughter, everyone turns round and gives them a wave. They look perplexed.

We'll organize you next, comrades!

More cheers. Ruben watches Maya grin as Sam whispers in her ear. Anna comes up and hugs Rosa.

MUSIC LINKS THE FOLLOWING:

A. CITY HALL

Maya, Ella, Ben and Anna hand out leaflets with other pickets. Banging drums and singing as they demonstrate outside the building as security guards fuss inside. (Posters: 'Luxury by day, sweatshop by night', 'No tax breaks for corporate cheats'.) Some refuse Maya's leaflets. She looks up at the faces of secretaries and other workers who look down from windows.

B. RESTAURANT

Sam, dressed in a suit, walks into a luxury restaurant and heads towards four businessmen half-way through lunch.

SAM

Mr Griffin?

Griffin with his mouth full of food.

Building manager of office block 646?

Griffin nods.

A pleasure to meet you!

GRIFFIN

Do I know you?

80

Sam nods at six volunteers in Justice for Janitors T-shirts who have just come through the door. Sam pulls up a seat beside Griffin and Co. Forks stop midway. The volunteers now grab free seats and surround them. Sam picks up the half-empty bottle of wine and fills up their glasses as he speaks.

SAM

Can you imagine working for $5.75 an hour, like the cleaners in your building?

GRIFFIN

That's got nothing to do with me! ... Take it up with their employers, Angel Services ...

SAM

Don't tell tales ...

EMMA

You're the building manager, you act for the owners who hire the cleaners ... so you take it up with Angel Services!

GRIFFIN

Who the hell do you think you are?

SAM

The organized working class ... Finish your broccoli ... it's good for your heart ...

GRIFFIN

Get the hell out of here ... now!
        (*to nervous waiters, who try to break the circle*)
Get them out ...

SAM

Calm down ... you'll get indigestion ...

Griffin jumps up, but can't get through the seated cleaners. Emma stands up and turns to the other diners.

EMMA
(*loud voice*)
We're just trying to explain to Mr Griffin that his janitors
can't support their families on less than $12,000 per year ...
Could anyone in this restaurant support their families for
this?

Faces go down.

GRIFFIN
You'll hear from our lawyers ... son of a bitch ...

PABLO (ACTIVIST)
(*with wine list*)
$120 for a bottle of wine! Are you finished with this?

*Griffin and colleagues burst from the table as the scuffling
continues. Sam grabs a piece of chicken from his plate as he gives
chase.*

SAM
Come back here, *amigos* ...
(*to the irate manager of the restaurant*)
Have they paid their bill?

C. UNION BUILDING

*Teach-in. Diagrams and analysis cover the blackboard, but now
every face of the fifteen cleaners studies a real video of genuine
footage. Ben, Ruben and Maya sit close together, stunned by the
images of the police beating up janitors with batons.*

EMMA
There were dozens of injuries ... twenty-two were hospitalized
and two had miscarriages, including my friend ... This took
place on 15 June 1990 in Century City, Los Angeles ... Every
year we commemorate it as Justice for Janitors day ... It led to
a big break-through ... After this, one of the biggest
contractors recognized the union ... In Century City today

we're about 50 per cent union ... health insurance, vacations and sick pay ... That's Berto there ... They broke his leg.

FUND-RAISING PARTY

Maya and Rosa dance brilliantly together. For once, eye contact and ease between them.

Huge poster across the stage: 'Justice for Janitors fund-raiser'. Jornaleros del Norte, a band made up from day labourers, perform on a small raised stage.

Glimpses of familiar faces. Juan and Ben try to chat up some girls. Sam drinks at the bar.

Rosa's daughter, Simona, dances gently, very gently, with Bert.

Rosa wipes the sweat off Maya's face with her sleeve.

The band belts out another great number. Maya skips over to Sam and grabs his arm.

SAM
(*panic*)

I can't dance ...

Maya pulls him.

Please, Maya ... I beg you ... Fuck's sake!

Laughing, she drags him on.

It's true. He can't dance. Ruben, pained, watches from the side. Sam and Maya hug tightly. Emma can hardly believe her eyes as Maya stretches up to kiss Sam.

Sudden screaming from the other side of the hall. Shouts of confusion. Sam and Maya run over.

SIMONA

Papa! Papa! What's wrong? Papa!

Maya fights her way through the bodies to find Simona and Rosa leaning over Bert.

ROAD. NIGHT

Sam drives Bert's old truck as fast as he can. Bert is slumped over Rosa. Rosa cradles his head.

                    ROSA
You're OK, baby ... OK.

Maya is in the front seat beside Sam. The truck screeches into a hospital driveway.

HOSPITAL CORRIDOR

A young doctor, who looks exhausted, talks to Rosa and Maya as they exit from a ward and into a corridor where they join Sam.

                    DOCTOR
... serious, but not critical ...

                    ROSA
What the hell does that mean?

                    DOCTOR
His condition has stabilized, so don't worry ... He was dehydrated ... It's very common with diabetics ...

                    ROSA
Excuse me, Doctor, what is the difference between serious and critical?

                    DOCTOR
There is some level of renal disfunction ...

                    ROSA
His kidneys ... Jesus!

                    DOCTOR
... and I suspect he has circulatory retina problems ...

ROSA

What the hell does that mean?

DOCTOR

Both eyes will need laser treatment at some point ...

ROSA

You mean he could go blind ...

DOCTOR

These are medium- to long-term problems which can't be dealt
with here at ER ...

ROSA

What's that mean?

DOCTOR

Emergency room. You'll have to make an appointment at the
diabetic clinic ... They'll carry out detailed tests on every
aspect of the condition ...

ROSA

We've waited months! ... And then they fucked up the date!
Now we've been told to wait another three months! We're
going in circles ...

DOCTOR

I'm really sorry ... but you'll have to speak to them ...

ROSA

Did you check his feet? He can't feel them sometimes ...

DOCTOR

Our responsibility is to stabilize the patient ... We've done
that ... We'll send him home tomorrow ... This is an
emergency room ...

ROSA

Who makes that decision?

DOCTOR
I do ... in consultation with the resident MD.

ROSA
I want to see him now ...

DOCTOR
He's at an emergency ...

ROSA
So he hasn't examined my husband, has he? And you're not finished your training and Bert's going blind and nobody gives a shit!

Young doctor's emergency buzzer is activated.

DOCTOR
Excuse me ... I'm sorry. I've got to rush ...

He starts running down the corridor.

ROSA
(*shouting*)
Come back here! I'm not leaving here till I speak to someone!

Doctor passes through swing doors. Rosa leans against the wall.

What am I going to do?

Distant noise of a siren.

VERANDA. NIGHT

Sam, Maya and Rosa sit on the veranda with drinks. Silence between them for a few moments. A homeless man with a shopping trolley trundles past and disappears.

MAYA
Will you sleep?

Rosa shakes her head.

SAM

How long have you been together?

ROSA

About nine years.

(*pause*)

I worked in a big house once ... Bert was there for three months doing building work ... I cooked his food and we got to know each other ... The woman treated us both bad ... One day she accused me of stealing her gold earrings and threw me out ...

MAYA

I never knew that.

ROSA

Lots you don't know ...

(*pause*)

Bert took me in ... I would have been on the streets. Didn't know a soul ... Later he married me so I could get my papers ... We got used to each other ...

(*pause*)

Simona was only eight years old ... He took us both in ... Then Luis came along ...

Silence.

SAM

He'll be OK, Rosa ... We'll come with you to get an appointment ...

ROSA

Have you ever been up there? I've written, I've phoned, I've stood in line ... Everybody's in the same boat ... How can you trample over a mother with sick kids, for Christ sake! ... If you can't pay you wait and take your chance ... Medicare this, Medicare that, a church here, a charity there ... I've tried them all ... How long's that gonna take? Too long! ... Cause he's fifty, fat, smokes ... White trash without a dime ... My Bert is a fucking useless nobody who counts for nothing!

SAM

I know what you're saying Rosa ...

ROSA

You'll never know what I'm saying!

MAYA

Rosa, *tranquila*!

Rosa gets up.

Easy, finish your drink.

Rosa leaves.

She doesn't mean it.

ROSA
(*shouting*)

I mean every God-damned fucking word! Stick your sympathy up your ass!

Her steps fade. Door slams.

Silence for a moment or two. Sam looks humiliated. Maya comes over and sits beside him.

SAM

Come home with me.

Maya shakes her head but takes his hand.

SITTING ROOM. LATER

Fold-away beds are laid out neatly in the sitting room. Luis and Simona are asleep.

Maya looks through the window and sees Sam's car disappear. She moves through to Rosa's bed and sits down. Rosa lies on her side, her back to Maya.

MAYA
(*all Spanish*)

Rosa.

(*pause*)

Rosa, are you OK? I know you're awake.

Maya pulls her shoulder round. Silent tears streak Rosa's face.

Maya lies down beside her and puts her arms round her. Rosa fights like hell to control deep, deep sobs within her.

Jesus Christ, woman ... let it out ... For once, let it out.

Maya pulls Rosa's face to her breast and hugs her trembling body tightly.

UNION OFFICE. CORRIDOR

Sense of buzz and activity in a corridor. Sam rushes from his office. An arm grabs him as he crosses with an older Director of Campaigns (tough and combative) and his colleague.

DIRECTOR

I want a word with you!

COLLEAGUE
(*to Director*)

Not now ... We're late!

Colleague walks on to the head of the stairs.

DIRECTOR

Three fucking injunctions in two days!
(*holding up one of them*)
What the hell you doing at night in Beverly Hills?

SAM

It's a free country ...

DIRECTOR

Not in Beverly Hills it ain't!

(*examining injunction*)
Singing, dancing ... what the ...

SAM

It was a lullaby ... for Mr Wallace.

DIRECTOR

Who the fuck is he?

SAM

Chief Executive of Angel Services.

DIRECTOR

And what's this about 400 faxes in one day ... jamming up his office ...

SAM

I'm trying to get in contact ...

DIRECTOR

Jesus Christ ... the lawyers are going crazy ... and I'm trying to keep some of the old-timers on the executive board off your back! And mine!

SAM

The walking dead ... they've woken up?

DIRECTOR

Shut it! We'll see what you're doing ten years from now ... Right, we got to think about changing targets ...

SAM

No way! We've been working on that building for four months!

DIRECTOR

And what have you got to show for it? Fuck all!

SAM

They're waiting inside ... What am I going to tell them? 'We've decided to look for an easier target'?

DIRECTOR

A better target ... with a better return for your effort ... Just remember who pays your wages ...

Director begins to move off.

SAM

Back to the good old days ... We'll collect dues, administer pensions and shoot the organizers ... You play golf?

DIRECTOR

Don't preach to me, dick-head ... Any more of these come in ...

(*indicating injunction*)

we'll be up to our eyes in debt, subject to a broad order, hands tied, snowed under for years because of your carelessness ... with not an organizer in sight!

Director's colleague impatiently snaps shut his mobile phone as Emma comes down the corridor.

COLLEAGUE
(*shouting at Director*)

Come on ... they're all waiting on us!

DIRECTOR

To be continued!

SAM

Venceremos!

DIRECTOR
(*walking away*)

I'll stick these up your ass ...

Emma waits for Sam. She looks furious.

EMMA

Before we go in I want a word with you ...

SAM

Not another one. What's wrong?

Emma stops.

EMMA

Your pecker! That's what's wrong! Keep that zipper shut! You know the golden rule ... no relationships between organizers and workers ...

SAM

I haven't done a thing!

EMMA

I saw you making out with Maya. At a union party!

SAM

She just came up and kissed me ...
I can't help it if women find me gorgeous sometimes ...

EMMA

And I can't help it if I want to kick you in the nuts sometimes ... You know it's disruptive and you've been warned before ...

SAM

I was drunk ... You can't count that!

EMMA

If it continues I'll see you fired, Sam. I mean it.

UNION OFFICE. DAY

Sam, Emma, Maya, Ruben, Ben, Ella, Cynthia, Dolores, Oscar and Juan sit round a table.

SAM

Angel have changed attorneys and hired the most aggressive union-busters in the country ... That's the bad news ...

EMMA

But there's some good news ... Those Hollywood lawyers you
have on the twenty-fifth floor ... we've just found out that
they are not just the biggest tenants, but 15 per cent part
owners of the office block ... We force them to take
responsibility for the way you're treated ... they can't wriggle
out now ...

SAM

They represent some real big stars ... We just got leaked some
juicy information ... They're going to merge with another
practice who act for some of the top talent agencies ...

JUAN

What the hell's juicy about that?

SAM

They're going to have a small select gathering ... only the top
people . . . to celebrate ... lawyers, agents, managers, maybe
actors ... some of the richest men in this city ...

ELLA

So what do you want from us?

SAM

We're going to gate-crash the party with volunteers ... but we
need your help to get in.

Uproar and shocked faces.

JUAN

That's juicy, man!

CYNTHIA/DOLORES/RUBEN
(*English and Spanish*)

You must be joking! ... How in the hell! Crazy! ... *Hombre!*
We'll get fired! It's suicide ...

ELLA

Listen to the man!

95

CYNTHIA

What's the point of this anyway?

SAM

Nobody fucks with the stars! Rule number one! Imagine how embarrassed the lawyers will be in front of their top clients ... Shit will fly! It's the best public opportunity we've had in years!

BEN

For a quiet life they'll put pressure on Angel to go union?

SAM

Exactly!

RUBEN

Or dump Angel and get a union company.

SAM

That's a possibility.

RUBEN

So we could still lose our jobs.

MAYA

Angel need this building ... It's their best downtown ...

ELLA

Sons of bitches ain't movin' ... They'll hang on like a dog with a bone ...

BEN

You're right ... It's a prestige building.

EMMA

We think Angel will buckle ... do a union deal. You get your health care plus benefits.

CYNTHIA

Millionaires! Any idea how much private security these guys have? Plus Perez and his crew, plus cops ...

DOLORES

Alcatraz, man. Cameras everywhere!

CYNTHIA

Even talking about this makes me nervous ...
(to Sam)
Remember how you screwed up last time ...

OSCAR

Easy, guys ... It scares me too ... I got kids just like you ... If
we get caught ... we're out ...

CYNTHIA

It's a criminal thing too ... Cops involved ... This is serious!

OSCAR

On the other hand ... when are we going to get an
opportunity like this again? For once we make these guys
understand they gonna feel the consequences too ... They
don't like that! They make $300 an hour ... My daughter was
sick ... I get the tests back next week ... What if it's serious?
... The way I see it ... I risk things if I help you ... but I risk
more if I do nothing ...
(holding up his hand)
I vote to help you.

ELLA

Me too ...
(holding up her hand)
I can't take that dick Perez shoutin' no more ... I'm up to
there ...

MAYA
(hand up)
I'm in ...

CYNTHIA

I'm not ... I think you're making a big mistake ... You're all
my friends and I don't want to see you lose your jobs ...
That's what's gonna happen! Don't do it!

BEN
(*hand up*)
We got surprise on our side ... but we gotta plan ... very
carefully ...

DOLORES
I'm sorry, guys ... I'm pregnant again ... I won't get another
job ... If my husband finds out I'm involved ... he'll go crazy,
man ... He hates union stuff ...

Ruben is next in line. Hesitation. He holds Maya's eye.

RUBEN
(*holding up his hand*)
I suppose so.

JUAN
(*hand up*)
Gonna get myself some autographs!

MAYA
OK. Let's work it out.

MACARTHUR PARK. LATER

*Life in all its variety. Swings for kids and football matches. Almost
100 per cent Latino. Maya and Ruben, in animated discussion,
walk through the park.*

RUBEN
I've got it all worked out ... I'll have the sixteen hundred by
the deadline ... with just $125 to spare ... It's that close ... If
I don't pay on time, next in line takes over the scholarship ...
They made that clear from the very beginning!

MAYA
So what are you saying?

RUBEN
I won't risk it ...

(silence)

Maya, I've been working for this for the last five years!

MAYA

We're all sending money home ... Can our families afford to risk it? ... Nobody can afford to risk it ... If nobody makes the leap ... nothing ever happens!

RUBEN

It's not just for me ... it's for you too.

MAYA

Don't say that, Ruben.

RUBEN

Maya ... I want us to be together.
(silence)
Well, say something!

MAYA

I don't know what to say ... Don't know what I want yet. I don't know what's ahead.

Pause.

RUBEN

What about Sam?

MAYA

I don't know ... I like him ... He's fun ... exciting ... and he believes in something.

RUBEN

And he's white.

MAYA

Fuck off!

She stops and faces him.

RUBEN

That's why you're doing it.

MAYA
(*furious*)

What did you say when Teresa got fired? Eh? Ruben, what did
you say?

RUBEN

What are you talking about?

MAYA

What did you say?!
(*silence*)
'She looks like my mother!' Remember!
(*pause*)
That's why I'm doing it! Because I had to give my first month's
salary to Perez and beg him for a job ... I'm doing it because
my sister's been working sixteen hours a day since she came
here ... because she's thirty-five and looks like fifty! I'm doing
it because Bert can't get health care ... him and 45 million
others in the richest country in the world ... We make their
food, wipe their asses, look after their kids, but they still don't
fucking see us!
(*silence*)
I'm going to study one day too. But what's the point if you
forget more than you ever learn?

She marches off.

OFFICE BLOCK. PLAZA

*Several enormous limousines pull up in front of the building. Well-
dressed agents and celebs are greeted at the carpet-lined entrance
and walk through.*

*Inside. Revolving doors. Dazzling smiles emerge. Flash of cameras.
They stream into an elevator.*

*The elevator door opens. Sam (smart but casual) and Emma, who
looks fantastic, are last out.*

BASEMENT ROOM

Ben, Maya, Dolores, Juan and Ella stand round a table as Ben summarizes the plan. Nervous faces. They stand round a detailed map of the building.

> BEN

Right ... We got an hour before they arrive. Any questions?

> JUAN
> (*to Maya*)

Where's Ruben?

> MAYA

He's not coming. We can do without him.

> JUAN

Que pasó?

> BEN

Drop it! Right, you all know what you're doing?
> (*pointing*)
Maya, you open the fire exits with Dolores. Ella, you hold the elevators, and Juan, once you get my whistle, you cover the cameras ...

> JUAN

Juicy, baby!

> BEN
> (*to Juan*)

Pay attention! ... I got the walkie-talkie, so I'll listen to what they're saying and pass it on ... Where's your watches?

They hold them up. Dolores has an alarm clock. Juan holds up an enormous diver's watch.

> BEN

What the fuck is that?

                              JUAN
  It's a diver's watch. Shit!

Panicked faces.

  I'm running out of oxygen!

                              ELLA
  I'm running out of patience!

                              JUAN
  Heh ... it's ten o'clock in Tokyo!

                              BEN
  Puta madre! Cut it!

*Dolores gives a loud 'shush'. They hear footsteps. Silence. The
footsteps pass.*

  Let's go.

CONTROL ROOM

*Dozens of monitors. The security chief lets out an enormous yawn
as he reads the newspaper.*

*Suddenly one monitor goes blank, but the cover slips. Bodies run
along a corridor and then Juan's panicked face close up on the
monitor before it goes blank again. But the guard doesn't notice
anything.*

OFFICE BLOCK. LAWYERS' RECEPTION

*The full works! Sam and Emma walk among the rich and famous.
A carefully coiffeured gent follows Emma with his eyes. Every
single waiter is Latino. An ensemble plays light classical music.
Acres of food decked out beautifully on tables.*

*Sam and Emma drift over to one corner where a half-dozen or so
people examine stunning blown-up photographs by Sebastiao
Salgado from his series called 'Workers: an archaeology of the*

industrial age'. Gripping black and white shots of thousands of workers like ants swarming up rickety ladders; a close-up of straining powerful calf muscles covered in mud; humped shoulders soaked in sweat and some poor unfortunate, bloodied, surrounded by an angry crowd and gripped by the hair.

Intelligent commentary about light and composition.

MIXED VOICES

... It's almost biblical ... where is it? I believe it's a gold mine in Brazil ... He works with some wonderful writers too ... He has a volume, *An Uncertain Grace*, with an introduction by Eduardo Galeano ... *Open Veins of Latin America*? Same man ... and José Saramago ... the Portuguese writer who won the Nobel Prize ...

Sam drifts over by Emma, who is being chatted up by man with coiffeur.

MAN

I've always been a horses man ... My grandfather had horses, my father had horses ...

SAM
(*jumping in*)
Tell him about your family's ranch in Mexico, Emma ...
(*to the man*)
She's too modest sometimes ... Excuse me ...

As Sam heads off, Emma gives him a 'you bastard' smile.

MAN

I'd love to see it ... How many acres?

EMMA

Not quite as big as you might imagine ...

MAN

And what might I be imagining, *señorita*?

*Sam keeps a careful eye on Freddy (security), who talks
surreptitiously into his walkie-talkie. Sam finishes his champagne.
Another is thrust at him by a waiter in seconds.*

> SAM
> No gracias, hermano ... Ya estoy medio borracho.

Waiter smiles.

> WOMAN
> Hey! You speak good Spanish!

> SAM
> Hey! You speak good English!

CORRIDOR. SAME TIME

*Cleaners run along a corridor directed by Maya and Ben. Just as
they turn the corner, they catch a quick glimpse of Marina coming
through swing doors at the far end alongside Petra.*

> MAYA
> Did she see us?

> BEN
> No ... don't think so.

RECEPTION. SAME TIME

*Emma, up by a little raised stage, has a few words with the
reception organizer, who then nods enthusiastically at Sam.*

> ORGANIZER
> Ladies and gentlemen ... we have a little surprise here ...
> Could we have two senior partners up here of the two
> merging firms ... Tom and Mervyn ...

Cheers.

> Tom, Mervyn ... where are you?

Sam takes the microphone and holds an award in his hand with a

velvet cover. A video team moves closer, as do the photographers.
So too do the surprised partners.

SAM

Gentlemen ... with unsurpassed brilliance you have
represented some of our best and most talented actors ... You
have no idea how happy I am to present you with this
trophy ...

Emma has a huge smile on her face.

At the same time as negotiating superstar contracts worth
millions ...

As he hands it to them, flashes of cameras.

in this very building your janitors receive less than $12,000 a
year ... Gentlemen, your turkey award ...

He pulls off the velvet cover to reveal a golden turkey. More
camera flashes.

'Worst Performance by an Attorney'!

Some on automatic pilot begin to clap, as others stare in
amazement. Whispers. A security guard sprints along the side of
the room.

But before you go, we'd like to demonstrate, free of charge,
what a superior job union cleaners do ...

He points to the back of the room. Everyone turns. Twenty-five
red-shirted volunteers have sneaked in, armed and ready to march.
In the centre are six huge industrial vacuum cleaners, which are
switched on as one, flanked by buckets, mops, brushes and dusters.

Freddy screams into his walkie-talkie.

Volunteers clean at speed, getting closer and closer to the
assembled crowd, pushing them back into a tighter space.

Freddy sprints towards the cleaners. He grabs a bulky volunteer. In a flash the volunteer has Freddy in an armlock, throws him into an adjoining office with windows and jams the door shut with two brooms through the handles. Freddy's furious face darts between the windows but nobody pays the slightest attention.

Screeching Hoovers now mix with Armani suits and beautiful legs. Soapy buckets and mops attack uncarpeted borders, splashing shiny shoes. Dusters everywhere. Other volunteers mingle with plastic bags, swiping away half-eaten meals.

Another guard grabs one of the volunteers. Another cleaner can't resist a rescue attempt by poking the vacuum cleaner between the guard's legs, rattling his vitals. The tail end of a shawl gets caught in another Hoover.

Fury on the faces of senior partners. Mixed reaction from the guests. Grins from two young waiters, who shake their heads in wonder.

UNION HALL. NIGHT

Party atmosphere. Juan moves around filling up paper cups with rum. Lots of cleaners and community volunteers, plus usual faces of Ben, Emma, Dolores, Ella, crowd round a huge video and TV.

Maya is at the back of the group with Sam. Great excitement and chat. There is a roar of laughter from all in the room which drowns out the newscaster. Shouts for hush.

On the screen a TV interviewer stands in front of the glass reception area to Maya and Rosa's office block. The red-shirted volunteers stand behind her with placards and banners.

> REPORTER
> (*checking her notes*)
> Business leaders have voiced their concern at what they call
> 'militant elements' amongst the Justice for Janitors campaign
> following today's incident in the building behind me. It all
> took place at a champagne reception on the twenty-fifth floor

hosted by some of showbiz's most powerful attorneys. They were infiltrated by janitors with military precision, which caught teams of embarrassed security locked outside. The unsuspecting partners suffered the indignity of a spoof award for 'Worst Performance by Media Attorneys' ...

More cheers. Maya moves closer to Sam. They chink rum glasses. They drink from each other's plastic cup.

SAM

We got to be careful ...

REPORTER

With me here I have Mr Edward Griffin, general manager of the building, and Mr Perez of Angel Services ...

Boos in the hall. Laughter between Sam and Maya. Maya secretly takes his hand.

GRIFFIN

(*shouting above the racket to the presenter*)

This is industrial terrorism ... No respect for law, no respect for property ... no respect for the police ... and no respect for their fellow citizens ... It has been weeks of hell ... They have blocked traffic, shopping malls, you name it. Nothing is sacred to these types! I personally was molested in a restaurant ...

REPORTER

Will you negotiate with the union?

PEREZ

They want a union ... they go through legal channels ... My superiors will never, and I mean never, negotiate with extremists ...

MAYA

Look at his face ... They're going to crack ... One more push!

Shouts of agreement in the hall.

BEN

One more push ... Hit them again!

REPORTER

Janitors gave their reasons for taking such drastic action ...

There is a huge scream in the hall, followed by hushes as Ella's face appears among a crowd.

ELLA
(*voice-over*)

We clean up after the most powerful men in this city, lawyers, Hollywood agents, bankers ... And I'll let you into a secret! ... They can't *count*!

More cheers.

... You can't live on 5.75 an hour and pay rent and support a family ... You can't squeeze two jobs into one day and call it life! ... On top of that ...
(*furious*)
no respect! ... Every time you see a twinkling light in one of these office blocks, think 'Justice for Janitors' ... We've had enough. Support us please! No Justice, No Peace!

Wild applause and they then break into a song.

Maya notices a couple of cleaners leave an adjoining office to join the group watching TV.

She grabs Sam's arm and pulls him to the back of the crowd.

SAM

What is it?

MAYA

Quick ... I want to show you something ...

Maya drags him into the now empty office and closes the door.

SAM

Maya ... I'm not supposed to be with you ...

Maya snibs the door and moves towards him.

Jesus Christ ...

Sam peers through the blind and catches sight of Emma.

There's Emma ... She'll kill me!

Maya grabs him and kisses him. Sam manages to break free.

We're not supposed to be doing this ... especially not here ...

He grabs her. More passionate kissing.

Oh, my God ...

Caressing. It's too much for Sam.

God damn it!

Sam pulls her tightly to him as he leans back against the window. His back smacks against the roller blind, which shoots up to the top with a bang.

Sam and Maya turn round in shock as they face the entire hall.

Fucking hell!

Instinctively they both duck down below the window line. Sam's long arm stretches up to pull the roller blind down again.

Nervous laughter overwhelms them both.

ROSA'S HOUSE. NIGHT

Maya, fast asleep, leans over her little bedside table. Her pen is by her hand. A short note to her mother lies by an envelope.

Rosa, in a dressing gown, comes over towards her. She picks up the letter and glances at it.

HANDWRITING
... did you get the money I wired down? I'll write a proper letter on Sunday. Bye, Maya. P.S. I think I'm in love!!!

Rosa puts the letter back. She picks up the blanket from Maya's bed and drapes it over her. She moves to the window and stares out at the twinkling lights of the downtown office blocks.

CANTEEN. NIGHT

Lunch-break. Janitors are half-way through their snacks. Maya sits between Ruben and Ben. The doors burst open.

Surprise on all their faces. Six new cleaners dressed in Angel Service uniforms come in and stand around awkwardly. Next come four security guards, followed by Perez. The latter locates all those he wants.

> PEREZ
> (*to Dolores*)

You ...

> (*to Juan*)

You ...

> (*to Ella*)

You ...

> (*to Berta*)

You ...

He walks across to Maya, Ben and Ruben.

> (*to Ben*)

You ...

> (*to Ruben*)

You got two minutes to get out of here ... before we throw you out!

Stunned silence for a few seconds. Ruben is more shocked than anyone. Sudden pandemonium as Dolores rushes at Marina and grabs her collar. Marina does her best to fight her off as the guards try to restrain her.

DOLORES
(*half Spanish, half English*)
It was you … fucking you … I'm pregnant! … How could
you do this? … *Carajo!* … It's you … I know it's you …
Don't lie!

MARINA
Shut up! Never said anything … What you talking about?

DOLORES
Fucking liar! Liar! Liar!

*In the madness, insults fly back and forward in Spanish, Russian
and English till the guards manage to separate them.*

*Other workers have started to shout at the scabs, who back off
into a corner.*

Maya looks at Ruben, who is in total shock.

*Dolores still shouts fiercely at Marina, who is equally rattled.
Marina tries her best to defend her reputation as she confronts the
room.*

MARINA
I've got nothing to do with this! I know nothing! Said nothing
… She's fucking crazy!

*The guards start grabbing the named individuals. One grips
Ruben.*

RUBEN
It's a mistake! I didn't do anything!

MAYA
Ruben! Ruben … Let him go … What are you doing? … Let
them go!

PEREZ
Throw the fuckers out!

MAYA

Please ... Ruben has nothing to do with this ... He wasn't
involved.

PEREZ

You wanna walk too? Get them out now!

Maya sees Ruben being shoved.

MAYA

Ruben! Ruben!
(*to Perez*)
He'll lose his place at college ... It was me ... not Ruben!

PEREZ

Shut up! Get them out and settle down.

MAYA
(*turning to Marina*)
What have you done?

Marina stares at her for a moment. Something dawning.

MARINA

It wasn't me! ... And if it was, why didn't I finger you? Better
look closer to home ... and keep your mouth shut ...
(*to everybody, shouting*)
Where's Rosa? Tell me that? Eh?

MAYA

What you talking about?

MARINA

Where's Rosa? Eh? Where's your sister?

Maya looks round the room for her.

I'll tell you ...

PEREZ

Shut up!

MARINA

She left two hours ago! After talking ...
(indicating Perez)
to him!

PEREZ

Shut the fuck up! Right, get them out!

MARINA

Who's gonna be the new supervisor? At the new building?
Rosa! Your sister Rosa!

PEREZ

That's enough ... Get them out of here!

MAYA

Liar! Liar!

MARINA

Just ask her how she got the job ... We all want to know!
Don't we?

PEREZ
(to Marina)
Shut it or you'll be out as well.

MARINA

No, I won't shut up! It was Rosa, wasn't it? ... Your sister...
(to Perez)
not me!

*Maya can't contain herself. She rushes to Perez as Marina
continues to taunt her relentlessly and Perez tries to shut her up.*

MAYA
(to Perez)
What's she saying?

PEREZ

She's fucking mad ...

> (*to Marina*)

Shut it!

Marina continues to taunt, despite the threats.

MARINA

The new supervisor who can hardly count ... Rosa
Montenegro ... buddy buddy of Mr Perez ...

PEREZ

Get her out! Now!

MAYA

No ... no ... It's lies ... It's lies ... She'd never do that ...
Never!

PEREZ

Get her out!

MARINA
> (*to Perez*)

Probably fucked you as well ... is that what happened?
> (*being dragged away*)

Who's got health care now?

At this Maya turns to Perez. She can see it in his eyes.

MAYA

No! No!

ROSA'S HOUSE

*Maya runs up the hill to Rosa's house. Breathless, she climbs the
steps to the front door.*

*She bursts into the living room. Rosa, doing the ironing, looks up
at her. They stare at each other for a moment.*

MAYA
> (*all Spanish*)

Tell me it's not true, Rosa.

Rosa goes back to the ironing.

I don't believe it ... I don't ... Rosa? Rosa!

Maya swipes the shirt from the ironing board. Rosa picks up another from the pile and ignores her.

What did you do, Rosa?

Maya pulls the second shirt away.

Juan, Ella, Dolores, Ben and Ruben ... Our friends ... Your friends! ... I can't believe it! Ruben'll lose his place at college ... He wasn't even there! ... Dolores is pregnant!

ROSA

Shut the fuck up! ... They were going to lose their jobs anyway ... It was just a matter of time.

MAYA

So you did do it!

ROSA

Yes, I did do it! ... And I'd do it again! ... I'm not going to stand back and watch Bert die on a waiting list ... Life is now. Now! Now! Not some fairytale in never-never land! ... So don't fucking preach to me!

MAYA

Rosa, listen to yourself! ... You turned us in!

ROSA

You turned yourself in! We think we're going to win! But we never do! Never! ... When will we ever learn? They're too strong ... They're always too strong ... How many times! Jesus!

A moment.

MAYA

What about Anna? She kept her mouth shut when we

organized the first meeting ... She's got a family too ... What about Anna?

ROSA

Anna's fucking stupid ... She should have turned us in ... She should have thought of her family first! It stinks ... but it's just too bad ... I don't make the rules.

MAYA

Rosa! You're a traitor! A fucking traitor!

ROSA

Oh, yeah ... traitor! ... Traitor when I supported Mama and the rest of you? Want to know how? I sold my body, that's how! ... For five years in Tijuana, every night, I fucked a stranger! Sucked their cocks! Otherwise you were going to starve! When Papa walked out ... Rosa picks up the pieces ... I fucked again! Again! Again! Again! ... Fuck fuck fuck ...

Maya is stunned.

Want to know how you got your cleaning job? Want to know?
(*pause*)
I fucked Perez ... I fucked him for you! ... Rosa picks up the pieces! Always have done! ... Bert gets ill ... pick up the pieces! You're right! A traitor! How many times has Simona asked me about her father? What do I say to her? 'You were born in a whore-house! Your papa's a drunk who fucked me for twenty pesos!' I can't remember his face! ... How many times have I lied to my own child? ... I've been a traitor for years ... a traitor to myself.

Maya is overwhelmed and begins to sob.

MAYA

Rosa ... I never knew.

Maya, wearing a cap, walks past fancy sports cars filling up with petrol and into the shop. She notices the TV monitor looking down towards her, and the teller behind bullet-proof glass plate.

As the customer in front of her leaves, she hands the man a dollar for some gum.

> MAYA
> Can I use the restroom?

There is a momentary hesitation before he hands over a key attached to a sizeable piece of wood.

> Thank you.

Maya walks to the back of the shop and heads for the ladies' toilet. She unlocks the door. A car pulls up outside but the shop is now empty. She goes inside and the door closes.

Sudden terrible screaming.

The teller hears her, runs from his cubicle and throws open the door to confront Maya screaming. She points to a cubicle.

> A body! It's a body!

The teller barges past her. Maya nips out and locks the door behind her. She walks smartly through the now open cubicle and opens the till.

She lifts up the plastic container for coins and throws it aside. She quickly picks up piles of notes as she notices a customer head for the shop.

She walks out calmly as the teller pounds on the toilet door. Maya confronts a sturdy woman at the entrance who hears the shouts and is on the alert.

TELLER
(*shouting*)
Let me out . . . open the door!

MAYA
(*shouting*)
Dirty pervert . . . I'm calling the police.

TELLER
I work here . . . Open the door! Help . . . someone help!

MAYA
. . . and get your clothes back on.

TELLER
Fucking bitch . . . I'm going to kill you . . .

MAYA
(*to the woman*)
We caught him in the ladies' restroom with his pants down.
Keep him in there till I call the cops. Careful . . . He's tricky.

WOMAN
OK.

Maya runs out as the pounding on the door increases.

You calm down and start behavin' . . .

TELLER
Open the fucking door!

WOMAN
And pull your pants up.

RUBEN'S HOUSE. DAY

*Maya walks along a street by Pico/Union. Multiple-occupancy
houses, similar to Rosa's. She stops at Ruben's house. He's on a
patched lawn polishing his shoes to a brilliant shine. She walks up
towards him. He continues polishing with great energy. She sits
down beside him.*

MAYA
(*all Spanish*)

Interviews?

Ruben nods and continues polishing. After a few moments Maya hands Ruben an envelope.

RUBEN

What is it?

MAYA

You'll see.

He hesitates and then opens it. He stares at a pink receipt for $1,600 in some confusion.

RUBEN

Is this some kind of joke?

MAYA

You start 12 September.

She hands him a little box. He opens it to find a beautiful pen and pencil set. He examines the engraving on the lid. 'Love Maya'.

If you don't become a fat-cat lawyer I'll never forgive you.

He fidgets with it and wipes his eyes.

Don't cry on it!

RUBEN

Where did you get sixteen hundred?

MAYA

Please. Don't ask.

RUBEN

Sam give you the money?

MAYA

He knows nothing about this. My family. My problem.

He hugs her. Juan comes down the steps of the house.

> JUAN

What's wrong, *loco*?

Ruben can't answer.

> MAYA

He's going to college!

Juan shrieks with delight and jumps on Ruben, hugging him and then giving him a huge slobbery kiss.

> JUAN

You're gonna be a brain surgeon, man! Gonna fix me up! Give me a kiss, motherfucker!

All three, tangled up, role around on the grass as Juan howls like a mad man.

STREET TO OFFICE BLOCK. DAY

An enormous banner, 'WE WANT BREAD, BUT ROSES TOO', drifts towards the office block, behind which are 150 cleaners and their supporters.

Sam, with a megaphone, skips along the length of the march giving encouragement and shouting out the chants.

He notices Maya in the middle of the demonstrators. He darts over to her and she takes his hand.

> SAM

Dinner! My house! Eight p.m. sharp! Cold champagne in the fridge!

> MAYA

And carry-out pizza?

> SAM

I cooked you something special!

MAYA

No te creo loco!

SAM

I'll send my driver round to pick you up!

He shoots off again as Ella digs Maya in the ribs.

Perez and security guards look through the plate glass of the reception area to see them move closer.

PEREZ

What the fuck's going on?

The revolving doors spin as staff come and go.

ERNEST

Oh, Christ. Oh, no!

The crowd charge the reception and sweep security guards in their wake.

Suddenly the noise reverberates through the plush granite reception.

With military precision the cleaners take up their positions.

They form a double outer circle and sit down. In the middle the mariachi band takes up its position and starts blasting out a number. Behind them Maya, Ben and Ruben unfurl the 'Bread and Roses' banner.

Other cleaners give out leaflets as security guards run around like headless chickens. They can't penetrate the double seated circles of workers, who link arms and legs as the band plays on.

Staff from the building begin to gather on the balcony, looking down on the chaos.

The band is in full swing. The more extrovert dance within the protective circle.

The band finishes amid a wave of applause. More spontaneous

chants, which totally frustrate the security guards, who try to shout over them.

CROWD

Heh! Ho! Heh! Ho! Union-busters got to go!
(*repeated*)

A real sense of community. Sense of fun and celebration. Witty posters, designs and banners. The first police on motorbikes arrive outside and peer through the plate glass.

Sam jumps up on to the plush reception and Maya hands him up his megaphone.

SAM

Over the last months I've seen you insulted ... fired from your work ... Seen financial crisis for your families here and back home ... threats of deportation ... families torn apart by impossible choices, and friends split by betrayal ... The truth is, struggle against these powerful companies isn't romantic, isn't easy ... I salute your courage!

Yes, we fight for our union contract! Health care! For holidays! For respect at work! But are we satisfied with a few more crumbs from the rich man's table? A few dimes above the minimum wage when the top 1 per cent of this country has 40 per cent of the wealth?

We want bread ... but we want roses too! All the beautiful things in life ... This banner dates back to 1912, Lawrence, Massachusetts, when 10,000 immigrant workers, mostly women, went on strike against poverty wages ... It was a tough, violent dispute ... but they won!

We don't get roses for nothing! We get roses when we stop begging, organize and demand a share in *power* ... When we organize a labour movement across the country that is strong enough to compete with corporations like these ...

>   (*indicating all around him*)
> that control our lives ...

We want justice, not only for janitors ... but for 90 per cent of the people, who produce this country's wealth but who only share a fraction!

WE WANT JUSTICE!

We remember the words of Frederick Douglass, born a slave, who died in freedom: 'Power concedes nothing without demand. It never did and it never will'.

We want bread ... BUT ROSES TOO! We want bread ... BUT ROSES TOO! *Queremos pan ... y ROSAS! Queremos pan ... y ROSAS!*

Outside dozens of policemen stream in with military discipline.

The cleaners see the police jog towards them.

The noise builds up. Dolores squeezes into Maya.

                         MAYA
It's OK. Easy ... easy ...

A policeman moves forward as the cleaners close tighter. There is the muffled sound of the police megaphone. Sam and Emma move forward to speak to them.

Maya stares at the line of police.

Suddenly the visors of the helmets are snapped down.

                        DOLORES
Maya ...

                         MAYA
Easy ... easy ...

The phalanx of police takes three steps forward.

What's going on?

She stares at their visors, faces hidden, police heads taller than short Latino cleaners.

The policeman with the megaphone ignores Sam and Emma, who have moved to the front to speak with them. Two other police start pushing them.

POLICEMAN
(in English only)
You have thirty seconds to disperse ... thirty seconds.

Suddenly, the row of policemen behind moves closer.

MAYA

Oh, Christ!

SAM

Sit down! Sit down!

All the cleaners in the middle of the circle sit down too and link arms.

A dozen police move forward and try to grab the linked cleaners. Pulling, shoving, resisting.

(through the mike)
This is a peaceful protest ... Everybody calm down ...

A policeman grabs Sam, who resists. Unable to retreat, he pushes back. General scuffle.

Police try to break the chain with great difficulty. Frustration builds, tempers grow. A policeman pokes a cleaner with his baton to try to break the chain. Scuffling and kicking. Ben, particularly stubborn, is whacked violently with a baton.

The chain is broken. Screaming, shouting, kicking and some violent blows from increasingly frustrated police.

A policeman hauls at Dolores.

129

DOLORES
(*screaming*)
My baby! I'm pregnant! I'll come ...

The police get closer to Maya and Ruben, linked in the middle.

Above, on the balcony, office workers are stunned by the violence, including a pale-faced public relations spokesman standing beside Perez.

Below, a cop pokes Ruben, who grips on. A second policeman joins in. Maya screams and starts kicking. She fights back like a mad woman as two police do their best to contain her.

MAYA
Ruben! Ruben!

Systematically, strength and superior numbers overcome stubborn workers, who are dragged and pulled from reception.

Above, shocked faces.

Screams, shouts and grunts begin to die down. Almost tranquil.

Dozens of onlookers above, in total silence, witness the last few cleaners dragged off.

Only the banner remains.

ROOM, POLICE STATION. DAY

Waiting area. Sam, Maya and a dozen of the other cleaners sit on a wooden bench screwed to the floor. Some are handcuffed to a metal bar running alongside the bottom of the bench behind them. Many have cuts and bruises. Blood on Ben's shirt. Quiet, downbeat atmosphere. Only 'police' sounds: computers tapping, camera flashing, handcuffs being unlocked and questions answered.

A couple of arresting officers are in the waiting area alongside the cleaners and finish off filling in 'field reports' they didn't manage to complete at the scene (personal details etc., which are handed in turn to other officers, who check the contents again before entering them into a computer). An aggressive supervising officer keeps a careful eye on them all.

Sam and Emma are being interviewed at the counter and their fingerprints are taken.

Juan, Ben and Ruben sit close by. An arresting officer moves over to Juan and fills out the field report on his knee.

COP
(to Juan)

You. Where you from?

(pause)

Yeah, you ... think you could manage that?

JUAN

Me?

COP

You! Where! Are! You! From!?

JUAN
(shouting out far too loudly, making the cleaners laugh)

Mex!-i!-co!

COP

Full name?

JUAN
(slowly, so the policeman catches it)

E-mil-i-an-o Za-pa-ta!

More smiles among the rows of cleaners.

COP
(to Ben)

Name?

BEN

Augusto ...

More smiles from the cleaners.

Sandino.

The cop turns to the row of cleaners, who are trying to suppress rising laughter.

COP

Think I don't write Spanish, assholes! I'll show you ...
(*to cleaner*)
Bueno, Sandino, Zapata ... Vamonos! Rapido!

They take their place at the counter to be interviewed.

RUBEN
(*to cop*)

Pancho Villa. Junior.

Cleaners can't control themselves. Lots of laughter and jokes in Spanish.

SUPERVISING COP

Shut the fuck up!
(*to police processing the cleaners*)
Right, I want every one of these comics checked out, in detail.
Anything comes up ... I want to know ... Right away!
Anything!

The remaining cleaners are bundled through from the waiting room into the 'waiting tanks' (one for men, one for women: they are situated opposite each other, and since there is no glass, only thick mesh, they can shout across to one another).

Sam heads immediately for the phones as he is pushed into the waiting tank. Juan shouts at the supervising officer who passes by.

JUAN

Heh, you ... Come here ... I know my rights ...

Officer moves closer as he takes out his notebook.

I'll have an eighteen-inch pizza with a mushroom topping ...

Peals of laughter as the rest join in. Sam gets through on the phone.

> SAM
> (*shouting*)
> Listen ... listen! I can't hear!

Shushes all round.

> BEN
> He's speaking to the union. Quiet!

> SAM
> Angel want to settle!

Some cheers and more hushes.

> (*passing on the news as he hears*)
> Benefits, holidays ... sick pay!

More excitement as the women shout across.

Health care too! We've won! We've won!

The male tank explodes. More shouts from the women. Theirs too erupts.

> SUPERVISING OFFICER
> Shut up! Shut up, I said.

Hands clapping and feet stamping. Embraces. Some yell in delight, while others, like Ben, hug a neighbour gently.

Men face the women through the mesh. Some are framed in smiles. Others in tears.

Sam and Maya get to the mesh and stare across at each other.

Someone starts 'We shall not be moved' in Spanish, and the faraway tank joins in. It builds up and up, till they blast out the chorus together. It starts again in English. Grinning faces, some

covered in blood, hammer out the song. Others are too overcome to sing but are there in spirit.

A cop enters and speaks to the supervisor, who is still between the tanks. They talk to each other and the supervisor studies the paper handed to him.

The final chorus ends. A cop tries to shut them up but gives up in frustration.

The faraway tank bursts into the union chant of 'SI SE PUEDE! YES WE CAN! ... SI SE PUEDE! YES WE CAN! ... SI SE PUEDE! YES WE CAN!'

Sam and Maya stare across at each other.

> SAM AND MAYA
> *Si se puede* ... Yes we can!

The supervisor moves over to the women's tank and calls on Maya. She comes forward and is brought out into the middle between both tanks.

Both cops speak to her now. Sam can't hear anything above the din, but he can see her face change.

> SAM
> Maya! Maya ... What's wrong? What is it?

Maya looks up nervously at him and shrugs. She is led towards another exit.

> Heh! Where are you bringing her? What's going on?

They catch one last glimpse of each other before she disappears. The supervising officer leaves and moves close by the mesh.

> What's happening with her?

> OFFICER
> We got a hit! Her prints match up with a theft at a gas station.

(pause)
Si se puede! Yes we can!

He leaves.

SAM

Let me speak to her ... bastards! Let me speak to her! Maya!

OUTSIDE INS OFFICES (IMMIGRATION). DAY

Dozens of bodies mill round the entrance to a yard blocked off by a mesh metal fence.

The group includes Sam, Ruben, Ella, Anna, Ben, Juan and all the well-known faces from the office block, who stand by the locked gate and attempt to peer in.

Sam writes a name on an envelope.

Ella and Ben catch sight of Rosa standing at the far side of the busy road. They encourage her to come over but she ignores them completely.

INTERVIEW ROOM. INS OFFICE. DAY

Dingy office and cheap plastic seats. Maya confronts an INS officer.

OFFICER

You'll be driven down to the border at Tijuana ... If you cross back over you could be prosecuted for grand theft pursuant to penal code 487a and if convicted face a maximum prison sentence of three years ... Do you understand?

Maya just holds his eye.

Did you hear me? You're dealing with the US Government now ...

Maya still holds his eye.

You're getting off light ... Consider yourself lucky ...

Maya continues to hold his gaze. Total defiance.

OUTSIDE INS. DAY

Sudden shouts from relatives outside the fence as they see their loved ones escorted in line on to a waiting bus inside the yard.

Maya appears at the end of a long queue and raises her fist. All the cleaners start shouting and waving.

CLEANERS

There she is ... Maya! Maya! We're with you, Maya ... You be strong.

SAM

Maya!

The gate opens and the bus pulls out of the yard. Sam and the cleaners rush to the bus. Sam stretches up to stuff the envelope through a top window that only opens a few inches. Maya grabs it. The cleaners clasp her hand.

VOICES

We're with you, Maya ...

As the bus begins to pull out Rosa runs across the road towards the back of the bus.

Maya stares down at her tear-stricken face but cannot hear her desperate shouts.

As the bus moves Rosa holds her palm to the window. Maya holds her palm out too. Hand to hand, glass in between.

The bus moves off. Rosa struggles to keep up as the bus builds speed.

Rosa stumbles along in the middle of the road till she collapses to her knees.

In the distance, Maya sees her being surrounded by Sam and all the cleaners, who comfort her.

Maya turns to the front and leans her head against the window. She grips Sam's letter in her hand.

FADE.

Credits

CYNTHIA	Melody Garrett
OSCAR	Jesus Perez
BUSINESSMAN AT RESTAURANT	Tony Rizzoli
BUSINESSWOMAN	Julie Ariola

CREW

Producer	Rebecca O'Brien
Director	Ken Loach
Writer	Paul Laverty
Executive Producer	Ulrich Felsberg
Director of Photography	Barry Ackroyd
Production Designer	Martin Johnson
Editor	Jonathan Morris
Composer	George Fenton
Unit Production Manager	Cathy Mickel Gibson
Researcher	Pablo Cruz
Production Coordinator	Heidi Pavey
Assistant Production Coordinator	Scott Fort
Producer's Assistant (London)	Alex Reed
Office PA	Rick Donatlan
Office PA	Kevin Keithley
Set PA	Rita Danao
Set PA	David Ott
Set PA Day Player	William Pena
Production Accountant	Cynthia Walker
Assistant Accountant	Jeff Wickline
2nd Assistant Accountant	Brent Petersen
Art Director	Catherine Doherty
Set Decorator	Melissa Levander
Lead	Michael Klingerman
Swing	Morgan Treven Bedwell
Swing	Jim Utter
Art Department PA	Paula Maslowski
1st Assistant Director	Ricardo Mendez Matta
2nd Assistant Director	Sharon Swab
2nd 2nd Assistant Director	Bradley Morris
Camera Operator	Diego Quemada

1sr Assistant Camera	Carl Hudson
2nd Assistant Camera	Matthew Pearce
Loader	Bill Olofsson
Stills Photographer	Merrick Morton
Casting Directors	Ronnie Yeskel
	Richard Hicks
	Steve Brooksbank
Extras Casting	Janet Cunningham
Caterer	Silver Screen Catering
Craft Service	Laura Gallo Colacilli
Construction Coordinator	Chris Forster
Construction Foreman	Scott Head
Head Painter	Eric Reichardt
Painter	Ron Cordy
Prop Makers	Ramiro Hernandez
	Tom Price
Labourer	Jose Morales
Gaffer	Marcelo L. Colacilli
Best Boy	David Bouza
Electric	Harry Gradzhyan
Electric	Kevin Cadwallader
Key Grip	Orlando Hernandez
Best Boy	Calvin Starnes
Key Make-up	Veronique Guillem
Key Hair	Yvette Perez
Locations Manager	Ken Lavet
Assistant Locations Manager	Quentin Halliday
Set Medic	Robert Allen
Construction Medic	Scott Baron
1st Assistant Editor (LA)	Richard Weis
1st Assistant Editor (London)	Anthony Morris
2nd Assistant Editor (London)	Paul Clegg
Editorial PA (LA)	Jeffrey Coulter
Property Master	Michael Lindsay
Assistant Props	Julie Sexsmith
Script Supervisor	Susanna Lenton
Security	CAST Security, Inc.
Sound Mixer	Ray Beckett
Boom Operator	Joe Brennan

Utility Sound	Richard Kite
Studio Teacher	Wesley Staples
Transport Coordinator	Lance Cherniet
Transport Captain	Roger Bojarski
Honeywagon Driver	Dand Blakely
Construction Driver	Gene Callahan
Driver	Reed Cohan
Driver	Sean Ryan
Driver	Claudia Ryan
Driver	Greg Dirado
Driver	Ron Bojarski
Driver	Daren Bojarski
Driver	Jay Gallaway
Wardrobe Supervisor	Michele Michel
On-set Costumer	Javier Avrieta
Additional Costume –	
Day Player	Ada Akaji

With thanks to:
S.E.I.U. Local 1877 Service Employees International Union
ELS Language School
Williamson-Dickie Manufacturing Co.
Reebock

Louis Rada, Jose Alarcon, Ruben Amavisca,
Alberto Betancourt, Garrett D. Brown, Jasmine Castillo,
Familia Cisneros, Andrea Dogendorf, David Huerta, Aida Lopez,
William Peña, Jovita Ramirez, Don Ranvaud,
Sebastio Salgado, Jono Schaffer, Stephen Soderbergh,
Grant G. Thomas, Gabriela Vazquez and many, many others

Chirla, Caresen, Sindicato de Jornaleros,
Sindicato de Trabajadoras Domesticas,
Casa de Cultura de Tijuana,
Departmento de Cultura del Estado de Morelos,

And special thanks to:
Vanessa Angel, William Atherton, Lara Belomont,
Cooper Campbell, Benicio Del Toro, Oded Fehr, Stuart Gordon,
Rick Otto, Chris Penn, Ron Perlman, Tim Roth, Robin Tunney,
Sam West, Stephanie Zimbalist

Through a Glass, Clearly

First Assistant Director Ricardo Méndez Matta,
on the Making of *Bread and Roses* in Los Angeles

If fifteen years as an assistant director had taught me anything, it was that all movies were made the same way. You schedule exteriors before interiors; when you move to a new location, you don't leave it until you have shot all the scenes that take place there, etc., etc. The size of the budget may vary, but the scheduling, budgeting rehearsing and shooting of every film are always grounded in the same basic principles. It took decades for Hollywood to come up with this formula, and I firmly believed it was silly for anyone to try and reinvent that wheel. But after a week of working with Ken Loach on *Bread and Roses*, I threw everything I knew out of the window and got ready for a new learning experience.

Ken wanted to shoot in continuity order, even if it meant moving in and out of locations. The crew were not keen on this; after all, they are the ones who carry the equipment back and forth. Ken would also not allow the production trucks anywhere near the locations. The crew weren't crazy about that either, not to mention the drivers. The cast had their own doubts. Ken not only vetoed the use of make-up, wardrobe and cast trailers, he would not allow the actors to have a copy of the script, because he didn't want them to know how the story turned out. Whenever I mentioned these things to anyone, I would invariably be faced with dropped jaws and wide-eyed stares. And there was my challenge: if the cast and crew didn't understand what Ken wanted, they could not deliver it. So, I wondered, how could I convince a sceptical American crew, used to the 'Hollywood' ways, to embrace Ken's European sensibilities and unorthodox style?

The best way I could explain it was that we would all have to stop doing what we do for a living so that we could make *Bread and Roses*. We are not going to make just another movie, I argued,

·we are going to embark on something very similar, some sort of cross between film, documentary, theatre and real life. When we're done with *Bread and Roses*, we'll return to regular Hollywood movie-making with great war stories to tell. The argument worked for the most part. Even though we still had some doubters, most of the cast and crew were visibly excited. But if I had managed to convince others, I myself was still worried. The schedule and the budget seemed horrendously tight, and none of us had ever done anything remotely like this. How were we going to pull it off?

Luckily, Ken provided me with the answers. First, he imported his key group of collaborators from England: producer Rebecca O'Brien, cinematographer Barry Ackroyd, sound mixer Ray Beckett, script supervisor Susanna Lenton, production designer Martin Johnson and assistant cameraman Carl Hudson. At first I thought this would backfire. The locals wouldn't like being passed up for the job, it would be expensive to fly the Brits in and put them up, etc. Plus, I thought, I'll have even more people for me to train the 'Hollywood' way. I was wrong. They trained me. Not a day went by when Ken didn't ask the production to do something that was outrageous, unreasonable and unheard of by local standards, but perfectly fine by the Brits.

Take our very first day of filming. The script begins on the US/ Mexican border at dawn, so Ken wanted us to start on day one, at the border, before dawn, photographing real coyotes smuggling our cast into the country. All of us, including me, objected. Why shoot at the real border when we could fake it at the nearby Tujunga Pass? It made more sense: the border was three hours away, we'd have to spend money on hotels, and we'd have to deal with the INS. I tried to talk Ken into it. 'Fake it?' he said, flabbergasted. 'Why fake anything when we have the real thing?' Needless to say, we did it Ken's way. We shot that scene literally right at the border, with a half-dozen crew members and without using any lights. The entire grip, electric, make-up, hair and wardrobe departments remained back in LA. I found myself chasing the camera up and down a dry riverbed, out of breath, in the dark, while looking out for rattlesnakes. I was hiding behind

Ken, who was behind Ray (hand-holding the sound recorder), with all of us scurrying about trying to stay out of Barry's shot. It was the most exhilarating thing I'd ever done. The Brits didn't even blink. They knew what to expect from Ken and were ready for him. I can't fathom how we could have done the movie without them.

Ken also brought along a great script by Paul Laverty, who had also written *My Name is Joe* and *Carla's Song*. The screenplay was written in the traditional format, but the similarity with Hollywood fare ends there. Ken and Paul were not interested in making a film about doctors, lawyers or secret agents. Our two leading characters were janitors. Not only that, they were female, they were Mexican and they spoke in Spanish! The city of Los Angeles is 45 per cent Latino, but you'd never know it by the amount of Latinos that appear on the screen. It took a British crew crossing the Atlantic (and the American continent) before our own story could become a movie. However ironic this may be, I knew no American studio (or network) would ever produce a story such as ours. You see, *Bread and Roses* is not about Armageddon, aliens or serial killers, it's about labour organizing. It doesn't have special effects, gratuitous sex or a happy ending. Instead it offers ordinary people struggling to overcome everyday problems. The cast relished such a rare opportunity to play truthful characters. They were also excited by their own process of discovery, as none of them knew how the story would end. Ken had Second Assistant Sharon Swab hand each individual actor just enough of the script for them to be able to play the next scene. At most that meant a few pages; often it meant nothing at all. The crew, on the other hand, had full scripts and knew where the story was going. Or so we thought.

The script featured an intensely dramatic scene between two sisters, where one forces the other to leave their home. As Ken always did, he kept one of the actors, Pilar Padilla, the one being kicked out, completely in the dark. She had no idea what was to occur in the scene. It would be up to the older sister, played by Elpidia Carrillo, to push her out. Ken loves doing this, he explained, because it allows the camera to capture a genuine moment of surprise, where the actor becomes the character. 'Why act surprised, when you can be surprised? If it works,' he reasoned, 'we've got it. If it falls to pieces, we'll just do another take.' But this time things did not go one way or the other. We began shooting in the morning, thinking that later that afternoon, we would film scenes of Pilar moving to a new home, once her sister had kicked her out. Elpidia worked the scene beautifully. She was strong, rough and brutally honest. But it didn't work. Pilar simply refused to leave. She couldn't. She felt such deep love for her sister, that no matter what Elpidia said or did, Pilar would not leave. Finally, after many tears, Elpidia gave up, probably thinking, We'll just have to do another take. After Ken asked Carl to end-board the take (he never says 'Cut') a quick conference with the writer was in order. After huddling for a few minutes, Ken and Paul announced that the afternoon scenes were being cancelled. What Pilar and Elpidia had improvised was the truth and they were not about to argue with that. Paul would spend the night rewriting the script to accommodate the sisters staying together. The rest of us thought about how truly magical film-making can be.

Had Ken filmed *Bread and Roses* in the conventional way, that scene would have been a disaster. In Hollywood, scripts are filmed out of order, which makes it difficult for the story to change course mid-stream, since the scenes following it are likely to have been shot already. You can make changes, and people do all the time, but not without great cost. By scheduling the scenes in script order, Ken hangs on to the luxury of rewriting up to the last minute, but without the expense. But how does one shoot in continuity without wasting time and money loading and unloading heavy equipment in and out of the same location each time? The key, I found out, was in the approach to cinematography. Ken never uses a crane or a Steadicam. We didn't even carry a dolly. Every shot in the movie was done hand-held or on a tripod. Barry used very few lights, sometimes none at all. We went through more than one shooting day where we did not use one single piece of grip or electrical equipment, not one. This made moving in and out of locations a breeze, which meant Ken could have what every director dreams of. He was free to shoot any scene he wanted, whenever he wanted to.

Ken would also not allow idle crew members (or unused equipment) to remain on the set. When you finished whatever you were working on, you were expected to leave, take your gear with you and not return until called for. It was difficult for some at first. But once everyone got used to it, it worked like a charm. The set was quiet and uncluttered. For the cast, it was a dream, because by the time they were brought to the set, all vestiges of movie-making were gone. No one would be in their sight line. There were no director's chairs, no video playback and no tape marks on the floor. The actors were free to move wherever the scene took them. The set was no longer a 'set', it was a real place. It was only fitting, since most of the cast were non-actors. Real doctors played doctors, cops played cops and janitors played janitors. Whenever an actor told us, 'I would never do it like this in real life,' the answer was always, 'Do it however you really do it.' Rather than bend the truth 'for dramatic purposes', the film adapted to the truth in the story. The dog would wag the tail.

Sometimes reality threatened to work against us. We staged a large union protest march at the Citibank Tower in downtown which appeared a little too real to the neighbouring building's security guards. It was hard for them to believe me when I said it was only a movie. All of us who live in LA have grown to recognize the ubiquitous movie shoots, with their maze of barricades, trailers and camera cars. When the alarmed security guard looked around our shoot, they couldn't see one truck or one foot of cable; surely this couldn't be a movie. They insisted we vacate the premises. We had real union protesters playing the union protesters, of course, which only added fuel to the fire. Before I knew it, my protesters (and my director) were arguing nose to nose with the security guards. I had to use every persuasive bone in my body to pry them apart so that we could go on with the filming.

Once we got past that, the scene progressed rather well. After all, we had cast real union activists to march on a building that they had actually picketed only two years before (the building had since signed with the union). Everything had been arranged for a smooth shoot and as far as the protesters knew, the scene was about a successful demonstration, a victory for the union. But what they didn't know was that we had arranged for the police to show up unexpectedly and arrest them. As the 200 or so picketers triumphantly sang pro-union chants inside the Citibank lobby, twenty-four of Los Angeles's finest (all real LAPD cops, of course) were deploying outside, decked out in riot gear and ready for action. Many of them had arrested the very same union protesters at a real picket only months before. When the moment came, Ken looked at me and gave me the signal to cue the police. Only a few of us inside the overcrowded lobby knew what was about to happen. I turned on my walkie-talkie and, struggling to be heard over the loud din of the protesters' song, I relayed the cue to the police. I felt chills go down my spine. When the police entered that lobby, the protesters were horrified. Some of them angrily and violently resisted arrest and had to be forcibly subdued by the police. After the first take was completed, the head officer, LAPD Lieutenant Greg Montgomery, informed us that the police were refusing to do any more takes unless the protesters agreed not to resist. Everyone agreed to that and we did one more take. It went down quietly and everyone was happy in the end, although I suspect the final film will use the first take. The truth always takes priority in a Ken Loach film.

Production Notes

by Iciar Bollain

Here I am in the United States, ten years have gone by since
I crossed as a wetback, with no identity papers I'm still illegal.
I've got my wife and my kids – who came so young they don't
   remember
My beloved Mexico, which I'll never forget and where I can never
   return . . .

Los Tigres del Norte

'*Bread and Roses* started at a bus stop. It was about two-thirty in
the morning. Suddenly I was surrounded by animated accents from
Mexico, Honduras, El Salvador and Nicaragua. Mostly women.
We got chatting. They worked as cleaners for bankers, insurance
companies, lawyers and Hollywood agents in some of the most
prestigious offices in Los Angeles. They made a strong impression
in their uniforms, as if descending like some army in the night,'
recalls scriptwriter Paul Laverty. Laverty was in Los Angeles,
according to Ken Loach, 'supposedly going to university but
clearly doing something else, spending his time with
troublemakers'.

   Towards the end of 1994 Loach was editing *Land and Freedom*.
Laverty kept in touch and in one of his letters he mentioned the
Justice for Janitors campaign. 'Several things struck me about
them,' Laverty remembers. 'They were irreverent and had lots of
energy. They also made me laugh with their stories, but there was a
real sense of direction about their efforts. Creative alliances were
being formed, with grass-root organizations, students and churches
coming together with the cleaners. There was a sense of an entire
community challenging corporate power. "No Justice, No Peace"
was central to their organizing drive.'

Loach was at once as enthusiastic as Laverty about the subject. First of all this was because the story took place in the United States, where he hadn't worked before, 'and I thought I should have a go before hanging up the viewfinder. It was also in the city which is the home of pictures and yet it was about a kind of parallel world, a complete other world that existed side by side with the movie world. It was about organizing immigrant workers, Spanish speakers, very vulnerable, easily exploited, and yet they managed to get over it. And having worked on the film in Nicaragua, this seemed another element in the same wider story, the relationship between the US and countries that are essentially its colonies, not formally colonies but in practice they are colonies economically and culturally.'

The opening sequences of the film show Maya crossing the frontier with other Mexicans, with two 'coyotes' as guides – essential links in the lucrative human traffic across Mexico's frontier with the USA. Maya, and with her the audience, gradually discover the other Los Angeles, this immense 'invisible', mainly Latin immigrant community. These are people who travel by bus in LA, who stand on street corners like the day labourers to get work – the people who do the worst jobs and get the worst wages.

'Spending time with organizers, I soon realized they faced an enormous task,' says Laverty. 'Many workers didn't speak English and arrived there illegally. Cleaning companies threatened them with not only dismissal but deportation from the US. On top of that many workers had two jobs, sometimes three if you include the weekend. They were exhausted. That, plus family commitments, made organizing incredibly difficult. For good objective reasons, many workers were too scared to get involved. For very good reasons, too, many workers were desperate to change terrible working conditions. It's a dramatic choice.'

Maya is rebellious, a troublemaker who, as her sister Rosa reproaches her, is incapable of keeping her mouth shut. Her arrival threatens to upset the precarious equilibrium of Rosa and her family. To make matters worse, the appearance of Sam urging them to take part in the campaign pushes the sisters to the two extremes of the alternative mentioned by Laverty.

But Maya's journey is also a journey into the family's past, into Rosa's past, about which she knows nothing. Thus through the two sisters the film explores the complex world of family relationships.

'The world siblings share is often riddled with a complexity which is hard to fathom. Secrets can fester. Loyalty and deep-seated jealousy can often sit side by side. Maya and Rosa, given their respective histories and personalities, make for a powerful cocktail where tempers must, at some point, boil over. But,' Laverty insists, 'I like them both!'

THE CAST

'We tried to look at Los Angeles in a way that was different to usual mainstream films or TV, in which it is portrayed as full of cops in fast cars and hoodlums,' Loach says. 'We wanted to wipe the mist from the window and see real people there.'

Ken Loach, Paul Laverty and their researcher, Pablo Cruz, spent several months interviewing hundreds of people in New York, Los Angeles, Tijuana and Mexico City until they found the main actors and actresses, as well as the rest of the large 'multinational' cast.

Pilar Padilla (Maya)

The Los Angeles actresses whose age and knowledge of English made them suitable for the role of Maya lacked the necessary background, naturalness and class-consciousness that the character required. Pilar Padilla, the young Mexican actress who finally got the part, did not speak English and so was not at first considered. However, during the improvisations that Loach carried out in Mexico she was the sparring partner for the other candidates. Gradually and quite naturally her presence began stealing the camera's attention until it became obvious that she was the actress needed to play Maya, a character full of fight and independence. As Loach says, 'Pilar is very direct and you can read her mind. She has great spontaneity and a strong spirit which blazes from her.'

After a two-month intensive English course in San Francisco,

Pilar arrived in Los Angeles to make her first film. Her previous acting experience had been in independent theatre in Mexico.

'Maya wants to live the adventure Rosa lived,' Pilar explains. 'She wants to be responsible for her future and help the family by sending money home. When she arrives, however, she finds that her sister is not as strong as she thought and that the workers' situation is tremendously unjust. She discovers that she "does not exist", that she is a ghost, working but unable to live her life without even a modicum of dignity.'

'I suppose Maya arrives kind of innocent,' Loach adds. 'When you first arrive from outside you see things quite simply, quite clearly.'

Maya's passionate character and rebellious nature lead her to join the union's campaign. 'For Maya Sam is a detonator,' Pilar says. 'It is he who opens her eyes, not only to the situation of her, Rosa and the other cleaners, but also to her own strength. When she joins the movement she realizes who she is and what she is good at. She realizes she is a fighter.'

Pilar revealed that working with Loach had been the best experience of her life. 'I think the secret is that he gives you confidence, a confidence that spreads throughout the whole crew. I'd always thought before that films were for cameramen and directors, not for actors, but now I know that for Ken Loach actors come first. With Ken the set becomes a temple. I feel very grateful – and very lucky.'

Elpidia Carrillo (Rosa)

Elpidia Carrillo became famous with her roles in Oliver Stone's *Salvador* and Tony Richardson's *The Border*. It was always realized that she was the ideal actress to play Rosa, Maya's sister, a generous woman made hard by forever having to fight her battles on her own.

'She's a Mexican woman who has had to struggle for work most of her life,' Elpidia says, 'so I can identify with that. Still, Ken wanted me to go to Tijuana to visit the *maquiladoras*, the foreign-owned assembly plants on the border, the sweatshops where the character worked when she was young. We also went to Coahuila Street, where all the prostitutes are. I guess that was the hardest part of the 'homework', something very powerful, sad and depressing.'

Rosa lives with her husband, Bert, played by the veteran American actor Jack McGee, a daughter, Simona (Monica Rivas), from a previous relationship and a younger child she has had by Bert. Her husband's illness and her paltry wages as a cleaner mean that Rosa has to do two jobs to keep the family's head above water. Since the slightest thing can upset the precarious family economy, Maya's arrival makes Rosa's life even more tense.

Living in Los Angeles, Elpidia was well aware of the immigrants' struggles. 'It's a reality that's right there and yet the Hollywood industry doesn't touch it. Most films are about action, with good guys and bad guys who are usually Negroes and Latinos. They don't want to show the dirty side of their own country, they don't want to say that there are many Tijuanas in Los Angeles.'

FILMOGRAPHY: *The Brave*, directed by Johnny Depp; *My Family, Mi Familia*, directed by Gregory Nava; *Refuge*, directed by Lindy Laub; *Predator*, directed by John McTiernan; *Let's Get Happy*, directed by Stuart Rosenberg; *Salvador*, directed by Oliver Stone; *The Honorary Consul*, directed by John Mackenzie; *Under Fire*, directed by Roger Spottiswoode; *The Border*, directed by Tony Richardson.

Adrien Brody (Sam)
The success of a campaign like Justice for Janitors needed people with irony and imagination ready to take direct action. 'As a kid I was rebellious, a troublemaker, and I got to use all that in this film,' Brody says. His character, Sam, is the least serious and bureaucratic union organizer it's possible to imagine.

His career has boomed recently. In the last few years he has made films with directors like Spike Lee, Barry Levinson, Steven Soderbergh and Terrence Malick. 'When this film came along I thought it was really different from Hollywood and Hollywood themes. It all happens in LA, but in a side of the city that no one sees.'

Brody admits he had lots to learn. In preparation he attended meetings, went on marches and spent time with activists, 'but the most beneficial was a weekend course in union organizing. I even had to share the room!' he remembers, laughing. 'They taught you there all the techniques about companies' scare tactics, going into house visits, assessing leadership qualities, who'd be helpful among the workers . . . basically tactics and strategy.'

As for his character, Brody imagines 'Sam's parents being immigrants and Sam seeing them struggling, and seeing the empowerment you get when you have some support. I don't imagine him as the college type, good-spirited, kind-hearted, the altrustic rich kid. I think he is more from a tougher blue-collar background. They are also more interesting to watch.'

'We saw hundreds of people,' Loach commented. 'The more we auditioned the more it became apparent it was a very difficult part to find the right person for. A lot of men who had many good qualities were maybe a little too earnest. Adrien has a sense of mischief and some idea of what the story was about. When you see him you like him, and that's important.'

Brody said he was used to working with a certain amount of freedom. Neither the way Loach shoots nor the presence in many of his scenes of non-professional actors was an obstacle for him. Quite the opposite in fact. 'It worked very well, because they've struggled in their own lives and can easily connect with the state of mind of the characters. Their truth can elevate your own performance.'

FILMOGRAPHY: *Liberty Heights*, directed by Barry Levinson; *Summer of Sam*, directed by Spike Lee; *Oxygen*, directed by Richard Shepard; *The Thin Red Line*, directed by Terrence Malick; *Restaurant*, directed by Eric Bross; *6 Ways to Sunday*, directed by Adam Bernstein; *The Undertaker's Wedding*, directed by John Bradshaw; *Last Time I Committed Suicide*, directed by Stephen Kay; *Solo*, directed by Julian Temple; *10 Benny*, directed by Eric Bross; *Angels in the Outfield*, directed by Bill Dear; *King of the Hill*, directed by Steven Soderbergh.

*

Two very important supporting roles are played by actors with hardly any film experience. One is the Chicano George Lopez, who plays Perez the supervisor, widely known in Los Angeles as a stand-up comic. His gags have a social content, talking about the Latin community and anything that affects them – like Law 187, which tried to refuse medical treatment to immigrants without papers. The other is Alonso Chavez, a Mexican who plays Ruben, one of Maya's fellow workers. His character does not want to get involved in the fight because it might jeopardize his college grant. In his own life, Alonso became a 'coyote' out of financial necessity. He started by entering the USA illegally in this way. He found work with an independent theatre company in Los Angeles and then helped the rest of his own theatre company in from Mexico to cross so that they could perform a play in Los Angeles. For a time he was a kind of 'coyote' Robin Hood, helping friends and relations to cross very cheaply and also helping them to get by while he tried to find work as an actor. *Bread and Roses* is the first film he has made.

Loach, as is his wont, used professional actors side by side with people who had never been in front of a film camera before but who had had personal experience of their roles. Thus Ella (Beverly Reynolds), a janitor, is the link between the union and her fellow workers at the racetrack where she has worked for seventeen years. Berta and Teresa, also janitors, are played by Maria Orellana, who has been a janitor for seventeen years, and by Estela Maeda from Guatemala, who has spent twenty-four years cleaning skyscrapers in LA.

The Mexican Roscio Saenz joined the campaign at the beginning in 1988, when the Justice for Janitors office in LA consisted of only six people. Roscio was Laverty's inspiration for Emma, the character she plays in the film. Emma is the activist who accompanies Sam on his visits to the female workers, on marches, to meetings – which is in fact exactly what she was doing ten years ago. When she was offered the part she faced a major dilemma, because of her heavy responsibility as coordinator for the entire Justice for Janitors campaign throughout the US. In between scenes she was often busy on her mobile phone or sending e-mails. 'Sometimes it was hard to distinguish what was going on in the film and what was going on in the disputes around the country,' she said, laughing.

Among the group of cleaners there were also men who have been political activists, like Mayron Payes, who plays Ben. An active member of the National Front in El Salvador, he has lived for some time in Los Angeles, where he works for CHIRLA, an organization that defends the human rights of the immigrants.

Jesus 'Chuy' Perez is Mexican. He has lived in the USA for twenty-nine years, working as a bricklayer, a carpenter, a cook and a hospital janitor. But he is famous in the Chicano movement because he is a singer and songwriter, 'songs that get people into the street to protest, because they use us here but they don't like us'. In the film he plays another janitor, Oscar.

Central to the film (as indeed it was to the Justice for Janitors campaign) was the participation of grass-roots organizations. Researcher Pablo Cruz spent the best part of a year working with them and identifying volunteers who wanted to participate, such as the group Jornaleros del Norte, whose music enlivens the party in the film that the janitors hold in their union premises. 'There is nothing worse than a bunch of bored extras trying to look militant. The people we found were real fighters,' says Pablo Cruz. Or as Roscio Saenz put it, 'These people have been doing that for years so they are proud to take part.'

THE CREW
Ken Loach (Director)

Once again, Ken Loach set off on the adventure of shooting in another country and with characters who basically talk in Spanish – as of course he had already done in *Land and Freedom* and *Carla's Song*. '*Bread and Roses* is about what it's like to be an immigrant. And in Hollywood, by and large, they are not represented. It's like the world of eighteenth- or nineteenth-century writers before Dickens, where the workers are invisible.' For Loach the immigrant question is in essence 'a development of the class issue. As somebody says in the film, it doesn't matter to the boss whether you are black or brown if he can rip you off. I mean, rich Americans don't have any problems with rich Mexicans.'

As he did with the group of militiamen and women in *Land and Freedom*, with extraordinary results, in *Bread and Roses* he set up a group of cleaners who would carry the story of the union's campaign. 'It was a great bunch of cleaners we had and that's important, because the strength and weakness of a film is not only the individuals in the main parts but all the life and vitality about them.'

Loach revealed that shooting in Los Angeles under union regulations was an experience full of contradictions. 'I guess you saw the good side of trade unionism, but you also saw the worst examples of trade unionism, which is when unions become self-protecting guilds. Then again, the Americans who made the film with us were magnificent – committed, loyal and hard-working. We had the feeling that there were many good people, trying to do good work, in an environment that was very alienating.'

Shooting in Los Angeles is very regulated, but not always in the most logical way, as Loach remembers. 'We had to be mischievous on occasions and break the rules quietly. Following their rules, or circumventing them or coming out of a different door from the one they expect you to, is always quite entertaining . . . like being the mischievous boy in the classroom again.'

FILMOGRAPHY: *Poor Cow* (1968); *Kes* (1970) (Karlovy Vary Award); *Family Life* (1972); *Black Jack* (1979) (Cannes Critics' Award); *Looks and Smiles* (1981) (Cannes Prize, Contemporary Cinema); *Fatherland* (1986); *Hidden Agenda* (1990) (Cannes Jury Prize); *Riff-Raff* (1991) (European Film of the Year); *Raining Stones* (1993) (Cannes Jury Prize); *Ladybird, Ladybird* (1994) (Berlin Critics' Prize); *Land and Freedom* (1995) (European Film of the Year); *Carla's Song* (1997) (Golden Medal 1996 at the Venice Film Festival); *My Name is Joe* (1998) (Locarno Film Festival People's Choice Award, Cannes Best Actor Prize, Danish Film Academy Best Non-American Foreign Film).

Rebeccan O'Brien (Producer)

'Besides being a great story that works dramatically very well, what I liked about the [*Bread and Roses*] project was the trickiness of it,' Rebecca O'Brien says. 'It really is making a film under Hollywood rules but with a European spirit.'

The road from the original idea to making the film was not exactly an easy one. From Paul Laverty's first draft of the script in early 1995 until the start of shooting in August 1999, the project went through various different godparents.

The funding was eventually achieved with pre-sales and co-production agreements with Parallax's usual partners, Road Movies Vierte Produktionem and Tornasol/Alta Films, as well as the participation of British Screen and BSkyB in association with BAC Films, BIM Distribuzione, Cineárt and Film Cooperative, Zurich, and in collaboration with Film Four, WDR/ARTEL/La Sept Cinema, ARD/DEGETO Film and Filmstiftung Nordrhein-Westfalen.

The eventual budget, around $5.5 million, was high for a European film, but not high by American standards, especially as the film was made under union agreements – essential for a film about supporting labour solidarity.

'The problem we had was that the budget under the American rules was too high for the amount of money I was able to raise, so we had a choice – either to slash the budget and make it work or to not make the film at all. We decided to cut the budget, simplify the film and do it in thirty days.'

Thirty days was two days less than it had taken to shoot *My Name is Joe*. This time shooting was more complex, with scenes with many actors and extras, quite apart from a bigger crew and more material than Parallax is used to working with – something else imposed by the unions.

Rebecca insists that she enjoyed the challenge of making a different film in which 'those who are usually in the background are going to be up there as the main characters on the big screen'.

FILMOGRAPHY (as Producer): *Friendship's Death* (1987); *Echoes* (1988); *Hidden Agenda* (Cannes Jury Prize) (1990); *A Statement of*

Affairs (1992); *Dispatches: The Doughty Street Papers* (1993); *Land and Freedom* (European Film of the Year) (1995); *Bean* (1997); *My Name is Joe* (Best Actor, Cannes) (1998).

Paul Laverty (Writer)

Laverty's collaboration with Loach on *Carla's Song* was for him the start of a second career after working as a human rights lawyer in Nicaragua for two and a half years and travelling widely throughout Central America. In 1994 Laverty went to Los Angeles and it was while he was there that he came face to face with the union campaign Justice for Janitors.

'It's comical to think back to when I first met the cleaners and told them that I wanted to write a story about their struggle – especially in this city, where thousands have a screenplay under the mattress,' he laughs. So, after a stay of just over a year, Laverty returned to Europe, but not before he had made a promise to the cleaners and organizers he had met during his research that he would return with a script to make a film. 'Bit by bit we got to know each other, but I know they still didn't take it very seriously, till they met Ken.'

Five years later Laverty kept his word. 'A labour dispute doesn't by itself make for a story, and you have to try and find the contradictions and idiosyncrasies of the personal. This story was much harder to write than *My Name is Joe*. I often felt several cultures removed, not only from the US experience but also from the many Latino cultures. It is a great mistake to lump them together. While characters might be cleaners and speak Spanish, the experiences of a Guatemalan peasant, an ex-combatant from El Salvador and someone from a shanty town on the outskirts of Mexico City are worlds apart.'

In the five years between the first draft of the script and shooting it, Laverty and Loach collaborated again on Loach's last film, the prize-winning *My Name is Joe*. Laverty is currently embarked on various projects, including a new collaboration with Loach.

Martin Johnson (Production Designer)
Johnson, who has worked with Loach many times before, admitted to a certain feeling of apprehension when faced with the structure in which people are used to working in Los Angeles. However, he insists that it was a positive experience.

'The only difference was that I am used to working with my own crew, we have known each other for years, and in Los Angeles I had an American crew. They usually have a different way of working, much more ponderous, more divided, yet the team I worked with worked together, so it was fantastic.'

Martin defines his work in this, as in other films, in the phrase 'I don't exist.' That is, his job is to make it seem that there is not an art department at all. 'Then we know we've got it right, and you can concentrate on the story and the action.'

George Fenton (Composer)
George Fenton has collaborated with Loach on his last four films: *Ladybird, Ladybird, Land and Freedom, Carla's Song* and *My Name is Joe*. He began his career as a freelance guitar player and moved on to full-time composing in 1975. He has received many BAFTA and Ivor Novello awards and nominations for his work on television plays.

More recently he has concentrated on feature films. His credits include *84 Charing Cross Road, White Mischief, A Handful of Dust, The Madness of King George, Groundhog Day, Shadowlands, Dangerous Beauty, The Object of My Affection* and, recently, *Anna and the King*.

Jonathan Morris (Editor)
Jonathan Morris has also been a collaborator on several Loach films – *Riff-Raff, Hidden Agenda, Raining Stones, Ladybird, Ladybird, Land and Freedom, Carla's Song* and *My Name is Joe* – as well as a number of documentaries directed by Loach.

He began his career in the cutting room in the late 1960s as a freelance assistant working on various feature films and television series. After spending eleven years at ATV (Central TV) Elstree, editing award-winning documentaries and drama for the network, Morris edited the highly acclaimed Emmy Award-winning series *Vietnam* for WGBH/CENTRAL in Boston, and formed a company that is now known as the Editing Partnership, one of London's leading post-production houses.

Barry Ackroyd (*Photography*)

For Barry Ackroyd, who has shot every Loach feature since *Riff-Raff*, *Bread and Roses* has been no different from the other films, despite the fact that it was shot in Los Angeles and he was working with an American crew. As always, Ken's rule of thumb holds: camera at eye level, with lenses rarely wider than the range of the eye, and with minimum interference in the action. 'What happens in front of the camera is always more important than what the camera is doing,' Barry says. This also means that lighting is reduced to the indispensable minimum, helping the natural light as long as the scene lasts.

Some of the intense, emotionally charged scenes are shot and reshot at length with small changes and tweaks each take, producing a shooting ratio that would be unacceptably high for many directors. 'Ken just lets the dialogue run on. With Ken you're never quite sure which bit he's looking for. It could be just a tiny moment at the beginning or the end.'

Loach is not after spectacular or cinematic effects, says Ackroyd. 'He just records what you see, like a documentary. He is always in pursuit of naturalism. He wants to get as close as he can to the feelings and emotions of the performers. That's why it really works.'

Michele Michel (*Costume Designer*)

Michele Michel, a Mexican who has lived in Los Angeles for some years, said that she really enjoyed the experience of making *Bread and Roses*; it became much more than just a job. 'It is like being part of a great adventure, not just making a movie but also learning about human nature through the story and the actors and the crew. Ken made me fall in love all over again with movie-making, he brought back the dreams and the pleasure of films. He brought back all the reasons that made me take up costume design in the first place.'

What made it different from her previous films, and in fact from the whole Hollywood industry, with its obsession with science fiction, terror, blood and special effects? 'I think that even the movies about real-life events don't really concern everyday people,' says Michele. 'I think this film will be a very good way to make people look around and see the janitors. The theme of this movie is about life and I think society needs to have a taste of real life in movies.'

Special thanks

The writer would like to acknowledge the terrific work done by researcher Pablo Cruz throughout the many months of preparation for the film in Los Angeles, Tijuana and Mexico City.

He would also like to pay particular thanks to union organisers Jono Shaffer, Rocio Saenz, and Triana Silton for their help, support and advice right from 1994 till the film was shot at the end of 1999.

If anyone wants further information on the Justice for Janitors Campaign or the US labour movement in general they can check the following internet sites.
www.justiceforjanitors.org and *www.labornet.org*

If anyone wants further information on other Ken Loach films, or Paul Laverty scripts, they can check.
www.parallexpictures.co.uk

I'm here to sing to you
about a sad situation.

Created by the White House
and US legislation.

All of us Latinos
suffer discrimination.

They steal our rights and harass us
with laws of immigration.

But I'm never leaving.
I'm staying here for ever . . .

I'm singing you this song,
so listen to me please.

It's always best to fight.
Don't stay on your knees.

We'll carry on the struggle
with famous words like these:

'*Si se puede! Si se puede!*
We can do it! We can do it!'

*From a song by a group of immigrant day-labourers in Los Angeles,
the Jornaleros del Norte, who appear in the film*

Let me give you a word of the philosophy of reforms. The whole history of the progress of human liberty shows that all concessions yet made to her august claims have been born of struggle . . . If there is no struggle there is no progress. Those who profess to favour freedom and yet deprecate agitation, are men who want crops without plowing up the ground. They want rain without thunder and lightning. They want the ocean without the roar of its many waters. The struggle may be a moral one; or it may be a physical one; or it may be both moral and physical, but it must be a struggle. Power concedes nothing without demand. It never did and it never will . . .

Frederick Douglass, 1857

(As a slave he escaped at the age of twenty-one in 1838, learned to read and write, and became a famous lecturer, newspaper editor and writer.)